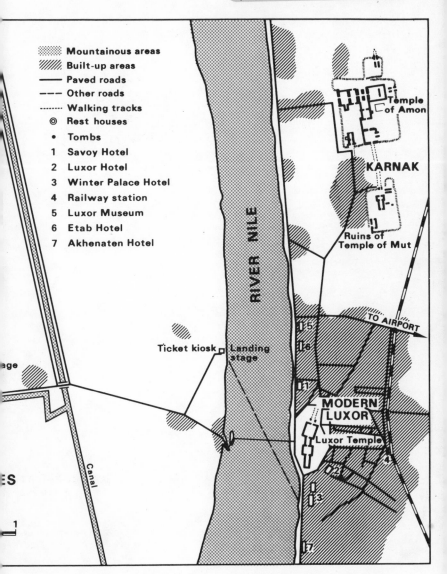

Mountainous areas
Built-up areas
Paved roads
--- Other roads
........ Walking tracks
◎ Rest houses
• Tombs
1 Savoy Hotel
2 Luxor Hotel
3 Winter Palace Hotel
4 Railway station
5 Luxor Museum
6 Etab Hotel
7 Akhenaten Hotel

RIVER NILE

Temple of Amon

KARNAK

Ruins of Temple of Mut

TO AIRPORT

Ticket kiosk
Landing stage

MODERN LUXOR

Luxor Temple

Canal

ES

# LUXOR

## A Guide to Ancient Thebes

### Third Edition

## Jill Kamil

Photographs by Alistair Duncan and George Allen
Plans by Hassan Ibrahim

## LONGMAN

### LONDON AND NEW YORK

LONGMAN GROUP UK LTD
Longman House
Burnt Mill, Harlow, Essex.
Published in America by
Longman Inc., New York.

Text © Longman Group Ltd 1973, 1976, 1983
Photographs © Middle East Archive,
and, for the photograph on page 31,
the publishers thank Mrs Hackforth Jones,
Robert Harding Associates,
who hold the copyright.

First published 1973
Second edition 1976, reprinted 1981 and 1982
Third edition 1983, reprinted 1989
ISBN 0-582-78339-9

Library of Congress Cataloging in Publication Data
Kamil, Jill.
Luxor: a guide to ancient Thebes.
Bibliography: p.
Includes index.
1. Thebes (Ancient city) - Guide-books. I. Title.
DT73.T3K35 1982 916.2'3 82-13965
ISBN 0-582-78339-9

British Library Cataloguing in Publication Data
kamil, Jill.
Luxor: a guide to ancient Thebes. - 3rd ed.
1. Luxor (Egypt) - Antiquities. I. Title.
932 DT73.T3
ISBN 0-582-78339-9

Produced by Longman Group (FE) Ltd.
Printed in Hong Kong

**This Third Edition
is dedicated with love
to my father, Victor Browse**

## ACKNOWLEDGMENTS

The author thanks Dr Labib Habachi, formerly Director of Field Work at Luxor and Member of the Institut d'Egypte, for his invaluable guidance in updating the text for the Third Edition, and for suggesting new inclusions and observations.

In the First Edition the author expressed gratitude to Dr Abdel Moneim Abu Bakr, late Professor of Egyptian Archeology at Cairo University, for his invaluable help and guidance in the preparation of this book.

The publishers are grateful to the following for permission to modify plans and maps: Hirmer Verlag, München, and Karl Baedeker Verlag, Freiburg. Also to George Allen & Unwin Ltd and Seeley Service Ltd for their kind assistance in locating the copyright owners.

# CONTENTS                    Page

CHAPTER 7   THE NECROPOLIS — THE
                VALLEY OF THE QUEENS

CHAPTER 8   THE NECROPOLIS — THE
                TOMBS OF THE NOBLES

*These are the official numbers of the tombs on the necropolis.

# PLANS AND MAPS

Page

**References to the plans and maps:**

References in the text to the plans are always in full: (Plan 14) etc.
*Italic* numbers and letters in brackets refer to points of interest within a particular plan. (*P.1*), (*P.2*), for example, always indicate first pylon, second pylon etc.

**Cover photograph:**

Karnak: sphinx-lined avenue leading from the ceremonial landing-stage to the first pylon and the temple complex. Photograph taken in 1971, before deposits of earth were located in the bedrock in front of the sphinxes. This has now been planted as of old.

# CHAPTER 1    INTRODUCTION

On the eastern bank of the River Nile, nearly seven hundred kilometres south of Cairo, there once stood an unpretentious village called Waset. It was no different from hundreds of others and as yet had no inkling of its destined growth into the pivot of a stupendous civilization. This was the site of ancient Thebes and of present-day Luxor.

Like settlers all over Egypt since the beginning of history, its inhabitants were superstitious. They lived much as they do today in many isolated rural areas, in villages composed of sun-dried mud brick houses separated by narrow lanes. Their lives were largely governed by the cycle of the Nile flood which they had learned to channel and to exploit. Because its benefits and its hazards came with untiring regularity, the lives of the people were similarly rhythmic, following an unchanging social pattern.

This enigmatic universe awakened speculation in the minds of the Egyptians long before dynastic times. The primitive dwellers of the Nile Valley, in Waset as elsewhere, devised explanations, at once naïve and delightfully imaginative, of the alternation of night and day, of the glittering heavenly bodies and of all good things on earth. The world as they saw it was created by supernatural beings who revealed themselves in the heavenly bodies. Atum, who created himself out of himself on the top of a hill that emerged from the eternal ocean, brought forth four children: Shu and Tefnut, Geb and Nut. Geb, the god of the earth, and Nut, the goddess of the sky, were one. They were locked in a lovers' embrace, Geb beneath Nut. Shu, representing the atmosphere, emerged from the primaeval waters and forcibly separated the two by slipping between them and raising Nut aloft in his outstretched arms to her new abode. Geb and Nut were father and mother of four divinities: Osiris, who became associated with the Nile and the fertile lands bordering it, Isis, Set and Nephthys.

The greatest phenomenon of nature, the sun, naturally made the most powerful impression on the Nile dwellers. Though universally recognised as the principal heavenly body, it was interpreted differently in different areas. The centre of the cult was On (Heliopolis) where the Sun–god was known as Ra (the solar orb) or Atum (the setting sun). Under one priesthood he was Kheper (the beetle), under another Harakhte. It was believed that he sailed across the heavenly ocean in a boat each day, from the pink-speckled dawn to the blood-red sunset. With the last rays of the day he transferred to a barge that continued the voyage through the nether-world, temporarily illuminating its darkness.

In these prehistoric times each town or village had a tribal emblem which was displayed on boats and flagpoles. The people probably believed them to be imbued with magical power, since they came later to be regarded as local deities. Their names bore no resemblance from one area to another. In the little village of Waset, Wast was the local goddess; Montu was the local god of Armant some ten kilometres south of Waset; and Amon, who was later to become the national god, was at this time either one of the eight local deities of Ashmounein, a district of Middle Egypt, or aspects of the fertility god Min of Coptos.

As time passed, commercial and administrative intercourse developed and largely incompatible beliefs no longer remained local. As a town or district grew, so the local deity extended its jurisdiction. The people consequently adopted a new deity and erected new shrines to him whilst maintaining the worship of their original local god. Sometimes a stronger deity managed completely to overshadow a weaker. This is what happened in Waset. The tiny local goddess was almost swept aside by the strong war-god of Armant, the hawk-headed Montu.

It is not surprising that the various settlements of Egypt should have tended towards political unity. They slowly merged until two powerful states came into existence: a northern kingdom which largely included the Delta, and a southern kingdom which extended south to Aswan. The rulers of the northern kingdom had as their insignia the *red crown*, and their capital was Buto in the north-western section of the Delta. The southern capital was Nekhen, north of the modern town of Edfu on the left bank of the Nile, and the rulers had as their insignia the *white crown*. Each state also had its own national emblem: the papyrus in the north and the lotus in the south.

During the long pre-dynastic years while these two capitals flourished independently, sometimes peacefully, sometimes clash-ing in armed strife, ancient Thebes slumbered. When the southern kingdom overcame the northern and the two were united into a single state, the people of ancient Thebes continued to live as did their fathers and their fathers' fathers before them: a simple rural existence where the annual flood was the all-important event of the year and the regular channelling of its flow the most creative activity. Little was known of activities elsewhere.

In the north Menes founded the 1st Dynasty and set up his capital at Memphis. After years of frustrated effort towards unity came the ultimate solution. The Pharaoh of Egypt was henceforth a god, the God-king of a single united country. And not only was he to be recognised as divine and worshipped as such during his lifetime, but his cult should be continued for ever after in a mortuary temple.

With King Zoser we pass from the *Early Dynastic Period* of the first two dynasties (*c.* 3100–2686 B.C.) to the period of the *Old Kingdom*, extending from the 3rd to the 6th Dynasties (*c.* 2686–2181 B.C.). Zoser exercised complete control over Upper and Lower Egypt. In his reign vessels over fifty metres long were constructed for river traffic, the copper mines in Sinai were exploited, commerce was carried on with the Phoenician coast, cedarwood was imported from Lebanon, slaves from Nubia. And he instructed his gifted architect, Imhotep, to erect the first large structure of stone known in history: the Step Pyramid at Sakkara.

By this time three different communities seem to have grown up in the area of Luxor, each of which recognised the hawk-headed Montu as emblem or deity. Armant, to the south, was the largest. Medawad was situated about four kilometres to the north, and Tud was a settlement on the eastern bank of the Nile fifteen kilometres to the south. All three were quite important centres for commerce, but otherwise of no particular significance.

Then came the 4th Dynasty and the epoch of powerful monarchs whose great pyramids at Dahshur and Giza secured them undying fame: Sneferu, Khufu, Khafre and Menkaure. Only a strong and effective government such as that under Khufu could have envisaged and organised, as we assume that it did, the erection of the great pyramid of Giza, by one hundred thousand men over twenty years. This was the development of organised society under one controlling mind and it was a period of unprecedented grandeur. But Thebes was hardly affected.

In the 5th Dynasty Egypt's civilization attained new heights. In particular her art reached a degree of perfection never known before. Commerce existed with Punt on the Somali coast. The quarries of Wadi Hammamat in the eastern desert were opened. The benefits were being reaped of years of intelligent, single-minded and imaginative administration. But then something happened that was to have far-reaching consequences. The unlimited power enjoyed by the Pharaohs was partly passed to their officials, and the result was an inevitable weakening of Pharonic power. In fact the 6th Dynasty saw the local governors actually shaking themselves free of the Pharaoh's yoke and establishing independence.

And Thebes? Political awareness was dawning at last. After the fall of the monarchy in Memphis there was a readjustment of the scales of power. This was in what historians refer to as the *First Intermediate Period*, the 7th to the early 11th Dynasties (*c.* 2181–2133 B.C.). Some of the independent kings in the north established themselves at Herakleopolis and others at Memphis. The disorganisation and weakness of the 7th and 8th Dynasties, which lasted for a mere thirty years, gave way to 285 years of Herakleopolitan rule in the 9th and 10th Dynasties when some degree of order was restored. Although little is known about them, the last rulers in the family line were powerful monarchs. And in the south power was seized by another family of monarchs, whose capital was Armant, neighbouring Thebes. Towards the close of the 10th Dynasty this family forced their way northwards from Thebes. Little by little they extended their authority, annexing local provinces and establishing themselves until the inevitable clash with the rulers of the north. The struggle was fierce and long and resulted in triumph for the south. Thus, after almost three centuries of disorder, Intef and Mentuhotep succeeded in reuniting the country. Theban supremacy was recognised, trade was resumed, confidence was re-established. And Amon was at last introduced to Thebes, not as a local deity, like Wast and Montu before him, but as the national god.

The *Middle Kingdom* covers the 11th and 12th Dynasties (*c.* 2133–1786 B.C.). The 11th Dynasty was Egypt's most prosperous era since that of the pyramid builders. The first Pharaoh over the reunited country was Mentuhotep II. Amenemhet I, whose rule heralded a time of great building activity and a literary and artistic revival, established the 12th Dynasty. There is hardly a town in Egypt, and Thebes is no exception, without some trace of the building activities of the Pharaohs of this dynasty. Goldsmiths, jewellers and relief workers perfected their skills, while architects raised some of the most beautiful temples ever known.

For some two hundred years Amenemhet's successors maintained a prosperous rule and Egyptian influence was extended abroad: along the Red Sea, to Nubia and Kush, around the

## Plan 1: NILE VALLEY

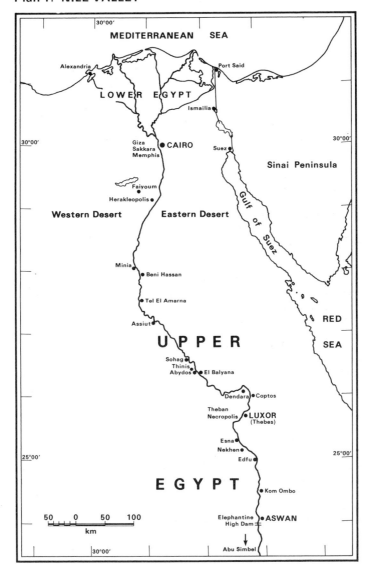

Mediterranean to Libya, Palestine and Syria, even to Crete, the Aegean Islands and the mainland of Greece. But though natives of Thebes the rulers had their capital in the Fayoum area.

With the passing of the Middle Kingdom we come to a time of decline, the *Second Intermediate Period*, covering the 13th to the 17th Dynasties (*c.* 1786–1567 B.C.). This was the era of the ascendancy of the *Hyksos*. Coming from the direction of Syria, these tribes occupied Egypt at the end of the 13th Dynasty and ruled for some 100 years until the 17th Dynasty. The Egyptian prince Sekenenre and his son Kamose finally rose against the brutal invaders. Kamose's brother Ahmose established the 18th Dynasty and the *New Kingdom*, which included the 18th, 19th and 20th Dynasties (*c.* 1567–1080 B.C.). He completed the task begun by Kamose, finally rid the country of the Hyksos plague and began a period of gigantic imperial expansion in West Asia and the Sudan.

It was only now that Thebes began to develop. As befitted a new capital, the expansion was slow at first but it continued with increasing momentum until the one-time village was transformed into the seat of a world power never before witnessed. Military conquests and territorial expansion went hand in hand with an artistic and architectural revolution of unparalleled grandeur. Following the accession and conquests of Thutmose III, who pushed the northern frontiers of the country to the Euphrates, booty from conquered nations and tributes from the provinces of the then known powers poured into the gigantic storehouse of Thebes. The greater part of the wealth was bestowed upon Amon who, with the aid of the now influential priesthood, was established as 'Solar God', 'The King of Gods', the great *Amon-Ra*.

The power of Amon was everywhere in evidence. Magnificent temples were built for him, elaborately embellished and adorned. It was both a duty and a privilege to serve him and successive Pharaohs systematically endeavoured to outdo their predecessors in the magnificence of their architectural and artistic endeavours. 'Hundred-Gated Thebes' was at the peak of its glory.

Primitive animal deities had long ago given way to variations of the human form with animal heads or, where the head was also human, adorned with plaited beard or characteristic headgear as distinguishing marks. Amon-Ra himself was variously represented: as a ram with curved horns; as a man with a ram's head; as a man with a headgear of two upright plumes in whose hands were a sceptre as a symbol of power, and the symbol of life. He was sometimes depicted standing, sometimes seated majestically holding his emblems. Only the Pharaoh of Egypt or the high priest delegated in his stead were permitted into the sacred sanctuary of Amon, or Holy of Holies. And only on certain days of the year was the deity shown to the populace, carried in extravagant procession along garlanded thoroughfares. Amon guided the Pharaoh in civic affairs, granted him victory over his enemies, favoured all who served him. Amon gave divine protection.

When Amon was dishonoured by Amenhotep IV (Akhenaten), who worshipped the life-giving rays of the full solar disc of Aten in place of the ascending sun Ra, this in retrospect affected Thebes but slightly. Although murals were defaced, shrines destroyed and the image of Amon hacked away, his dethronement was short-lived. Tutankhamon, on succeeding to the throne, started the restoration of damaged temples, and Haremhab, Ramses I, Seti I and Ramses II continued the work of rebuilding, reconstructing and renovating the temples, to restore the reputation of the King of Gods.

Down the years Amon's wealth increased enormously. He possessed over 5,000 divine statues, more than 81,000 slaves, vassals and servants, well over 421,000 head of cattle, 433 gardens and orchards, 691,334 acres of land, 83 ships, 46 building yards and 65 cities and towns.[1]

The arch-priests, already wielding a growing political power as a result of their very special reinstated position, gradually came to regard themselves as the ruling power of the state. Their long-awaited opportunity finally came when Akhenaten's religious revolt was followed, in the 20th Dynasty, by a succession of weak rulers. This enabled Amon's priests to usurp the throne and for a time to unite priesthood with royalty. The days of Egyptian conquest were over.

To endeavour to date the fall of Thebes is difficult. One could say it started as far back as the 18th Dynasty when Akhenaten, the sensitive, peace-loving Pharaoh who believed in a universal god, shifted the capital to Tel el Amarna and failed to maintain his foreign interests. One could date it to the reign of Ramses II in the 19th Dynasty when, in his concern to place his armies more strategically for his battles against the Hittites, he transferred the royal residence to Per-Ramses in the eastern part of the Delta. Or one could see the 20th Dynasty as the turning point, and certainly Ramses III and his ever-weakening successors fell more and more under the yoke of the priesthood and undoubtedly contributed to the collapse of the state. But the real downward slope of the graph, and its continued drop, came in the 21st Dynasty, just over one

[1] *Harris Papyrus* written during the reign of Ramses III.

thousand years B.C., when Hrihor made Egypt an ecclesiastical state. Thus began the period known by historians as the *Period of Decline* of the 21st to the 24th Dynasties (*c.* 1080–715 B.C.) followed by the *Late Period*, the 25th to 30th Dynasties (*c.* 750–332 B.C.).

Nubia took advantage of the weakened capital to gain independence. Palestine and Syria were lost. The throne was then usurped by Libyan monarchs who ruled for nearly two hundred years. They were in turn ousted by the Kushites. The growing Assyrian empire advanced on Egypt, plundering the capital and overthrowing the Kushite rulers. And though the country shook off the occupying forces during a short-lived comeback under the kings of the 26th Dynasty, the Persians invaded Egypt in 525 B.C. and the country became a Persian province. Then Alexander the Great marched triumphantly along the Nile Valley to liberate the country but actually succeeded in destroying the state's independent status once and for all. Finally the Romans turned Egypt into a colony.

Yet while Thebes was sinking into mediocrity, its conquerors treated it as a great city and tried to preserve and embellish it. The Kushites particularly, having assimilated the culture of Egypt and become fanatical adherents of Amon, sought to reinspire Theban culture and safeguard the city from collapse. The kings of the 26th Dynasty built lesser temples to Amon and bestowed their wealth, what remained of it, upon him. The invading army of Cambyses, though striking as far as Upper Egypt, actually did very little damage to the city. The rule of the Ptolemies is noted for its architectural activity and the Greeks conscientiously endeavoured to add to the splendour of national buildings after a priest had told Alexander that he was the son of Amon and should revere him. The Romans too repaired ruins and built temples in the traditional style, each retaining something of the earlier grandeur. But it was a losing battle. The past was not to be recaptured. Thebes could hardly hide its well-earned wrinkles and a time-weathered quality lay over the metropolis.

With the advent of the divine religions came systematic destruction. It happened first in the tombs and shrines where the early Christians hid. Later the 'pagan' statues were uprooted, sacred sanctuaries mutilated, attempts made to topple obelisks and colossi and obliterate forever the visages of the 'heathen gods'. Akhenaten's acts were half-hearted dabblings when compared with this wholesale destruction. The city weakened and crumbled till it was no more than a collection of villages.

At last, as though wishing to protect what remained, the dry desert winds blew a mantle of sand over the dead city. Particle settled firmly onto particle, layer upon layer, until once lofty colonnades were half submerged in a sea of sand. Between the elaborately decorated capitals childrens' playgrounds sprang up. Mud dwellings were built by peasants alongside sculptured wall and column. Dovecots were erected on architrave and pylon. Ancient Thebes was gone. 'Luxor' was born: its name being derived from the Arabic *El-Oksor*, 'the palaces'.

Still the destruction went on. Slabs from the monuments with their invaluable inscriptions were torn down or reduced to lime. Wind and sun ate into the façades. And the Nile, rising and falling with the annual flood, continued to play its part in causing irreparable harm to the treasures of Amon.

It was left to the modern archeologists, who began to filter southwards before the turn of the 19th century, to excavate and interpret for us the golden era of Egypt's history.

Napoleon Bonaparte unlocked the door to the past. His 1798 expedition to Egypt, while militarily disappointing in its failure to wrench political power from the British, remains significant for its impressive archeological research and for the establishment of the *Institut d'Egypte* in Cairo. In fact it was to the Institut that the famous *Rosetta Stone*, discovered by soldiers digging a trench near the fortress of St. Julian at Rosetta, was sent. This stone was quickly recognised as some sort of decree written in three scripts and thus a possible key to the understanding of the 'picture language' which had been lost since the days of the Roman occupation. The bottom text was in Greek. At the top of the stone was the sacred Egyptian 'symbol writing', understood only by the priests, and in between the two was the popular script which was understood by the masses. However, the texts had to wait a full twenty years, until 1822, to be deciphered. The French scholar Jean François Champollion who worked on them for ten years finally established that, far from the hieroglyphics being symbols as was supposed, each picture actually represented a phonetic sound which, combined, spelled out words. Champollion compiled a dictionary of the lost language. It is thanks to him that we have an insight into the ancient religion, the manners and the customs of a people of long ago and, above all, into the complex political institutions of a civilization that endured for five thousand years.

For many years excavation was dominated by the French. Loret was responsible for discovering the tombs of Thutmose III, Amenhotep II and Ramses I. Belzoni excavated the tomb that surpasses all others in size and artistic execution, that of Seti I. In 1820 he said that in his opinion there were no more tombs to be found in the Valley of the Kings. The French also gave Egypt Mariette, who revealed the delicately carved reliefs of Queen Hatshepsut's voyage to the Land of Punt, and Maspero, who was in charge of the Egyptian Department of Antiquities for many years.

As early as 1844 German expeditions were making such important finds as the tombs of Ramses II and Merneptah. Then in 1881 Emil Brugsch, following a local rumour, discovered the 'cache' or 'shaft' at Deir el Bahri, containing a hoard of mummies of some of Egypt's most important Pharaohs, hidden there for safety from tomb-robbers by the priests of the 21st Dynasty. This fantastic discovery started an avalanche of interest in Egyptology. England's Flinders Petrie worked with his teams in the mortuary temples for many years. Italy's Professor Schiaparelli excavated enthusiastically in the Valley of the Queens, and T. M. Davis, the wealthy American who excavated on the necropolis, said in 1912 what Belzoni had said before him, that the Valley of the Kings was now exhausted. Then came Howard Carter and the most extraordinary discovery of all: the almost intact tomb of Tutankhamon, discovered in 1922.

A recent significant discovery was made in the spring of 1976: Egyptologists digging at a site to the east of the Great Temple of Amon at Karnak, unearthed the foundations of a long wall and fragments of relief which identify it as the long sought site of one of Akhenaten's Sun Temples. With today's modern techniques, perhaps we shall find that the revelations of ancient Egypt have only just begun. Certainly we are becoming more aware of the ancient Egyptian predilection for scientific accuracy: on the inner surface of the ear of an animal — probably a hyena — depicted in a tomb at Dra Abu el Naga, are three ovals. It has been suggested that these are feeding ticks, and that they are probably the adults of a common parasite in the Nile valley, known as the brown dog-tick.

As we show in our concluding chapter, work continues today on both sides of the Nile at Luxor.

**Plan 2**

**LUXOR TEMPLE**

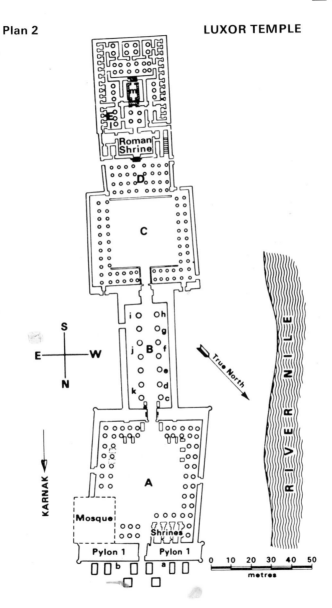

## CHAPTER 2    THE TEMPLE OF LUXOR

### BACKGROUND

Amenhotep III, the 18th Dynasty Pharaoh and great-grandson of the military genius Thutmose III, built the temple of Luxor close to the banks of the Nile just south of the city. Though by this time Egyptian military power was past its peak, economic conditions within the capital were sound. Trade was flourishing with wealth pouring in from the distant provinces of the empire, which comprised almost all West Asia including Palestine, Syria, Phoenicia, the western part of the Euphrates, Nubia, Kush and Libya. Extravagant caravans brought gold and silver, metalware, ivory and timber, spices for the royal taste and strange and exotic animals to roam in private gardens. The temples were bursting with tributes, walls and columns were encrusted with richness and colour, feasts and festivals were bountiful, the pace was brisk, the mood content.

Amenhotep ruled in splendour with relatively little to concern him politically apart from a Nubian revolt which was quickly quelled. His Asian supremacy was unchallenged and he was confident that his armies were strong enough to maintain his foreign empire. At home his viziers took care of all matters of state and held the reins of power in their able hands.

Advantage was taken of slave labour from Nubia and Asia, and Amenhotep imbued traditional architecture with new life both by enlarging and embellishing existing temples and also by building new ones. Apart from the Luxor temple he completed the temple to Mut, in the great Karnak triad (page 65), which had been begun by his ancestors, giving it grace and elegance. Size was no deterrent, as can be gauged from the statues at the entrance to his mortuary temple on the necropolis, now known as the Colossi of Memnon (page 100).

This was perhaps the most trouble-free time in Egyptian history. The country was united, the nightmare rule of the Hyksos was no more than a bad memory. The empire was expansive, slave labour cheap, wealth abundant and Amenhotep had every reason to be the most carefree of Pharaohs. He raised his bow to beasts and fowl on his native soil where his ancestors had raised theirs to the enemy on alien lands. His wife, Queen Tiy, was very beautiful and clearly loved by the Pharaoh, as she is depicted in name or person always at his side and far more frequently than was usual for royal wives of earlier rulers.

In the circumstances it is not surprising that Amenhotep, architecturally active and emotionally content, should have developed an interest in horticulture. Near his palace on the necropolis his enormous artificial lake, over 1,700 metres long and 500 wide, was surrounded by luxuriant foliage. Between the temple of Luxor and that of Karnak he laid out beautiful gardens, lining the avenue with rams carved in stone, each with a statue of himself between its forepaws. The effect must have been one of overwhelming grandeur as solemn processions and dazzling ceremonies passed along this splendid avenue.

At Karnak Amenhotep III continued the new theme in architecture: the *pylon*, a huge stone tower sloping inwards from the base. A pylon stood on each side of the entrance to the temple. Thebes was never to know better; bigger, maybe, but never better.

'Isis' anchors beside Luxor Temple.

Because the temple of Luxor, like that of Karnak and in fact like most other temples throughout the land, was built not by a single architect or according to a uniform plan, but reflected the ideas and whims of many successive rulers, it is necessary before describing the first pylon, which was actually the last addition to the temple, to have some idea of how it developed, underwent alteration, appropriation, calculated destruction and, finally, excavation.

The temple was constructed on the site of a small temple to Amon built by the Pharaohs of the 12th Dynasty. Amenhotep III had his architects rebuild the modest original sanctuary which was as always the first part of the temple to be built, renovate the surrounding chambers and design a forecourt of fine, slender colonnades. It is this court, with its clustered papyrus-bud columns, that can be seen from the Nile and that gives the temple its special character.

It was planned along traditional lines. Like all Egyptian temples it had a sanctuary or Holy of Holies with surrounding chambers, a large colonnaded hall — the *hypostyle* hall (Plan 2 D)—and an open court (C). A second court was also planned but only the huge columns of the nave were erected before the death of the Pharaoh. His son Amenhotep IV, who later became known as Akhenaten and transferred the royal residence to Tel el Amarna, was far too hostile towards Amon to complete the work. At his time the temple was only 190 metres long and 55 metres wide at its greatest span. Three small granite shrines, which had been erected by Hatshepsut and usurped by Thutmose III, stood opposite the entrance.

And then came the first of a long series of changes. During the religious revolution under Amenhotep IV the temple was stripped of the images and names of the ancient deities, especially those relating to Amon, who even disappeared from the divine sign that included the name of the Pharaoh, the oval *cartouche*.

Akhenaten's successor, Tutankhamon, transferred the royal residence back to Thebes. The wall reliefs of the Luxor temple were inscribed with his name only to be changed again to that of his successor Haremhab. It was probably Tutankhamon who had the walls erected on each side of the columns of the unfinished court (B) and had the inner surfaces inscribed with reliefs.

In the 19th Dynasty Seti I made a concerted effort to continue the restoration of the worship of Amon but added nothing to the temple's architecture. The major alterations were left to that great Pharonic builder and most celebrated of Egyptian kings, Ramses II. His large colonnaded court (A) was placed before the temple of his ancestors and he usurped the shrines of Thutmose III, altering the reliefs to bear his own name. He also erected a massive pylon, two obelisks and six colossal statues of himself at the northern end of the temple, thus forming an impressive entrance to the whole complex. The temple was now 260 metres long.

Few further alterations took place until the advent of Christianity, when the entire area between the sanctuary and the hypostyle hall was converted into a Roman shrine where early Christians had to make offerings to four Christian emperors. The wall representations were plastered over and where the plaster has fallen off we can see a jig-saw of Roman Emperors and ancient gods.

One of the chambers adjoining the sanctuary, which was restored by Alexander the Great, was inhabited by the engineer who supervised the transportation of the pink granite obelisk from the entrance of the temple to the Place de la Concorde in Paris. It was the French who first started serious excavations of the Luxor temple and who cleared most of the mediaeval buildings about it. The exception is the Mosque of Abu el Hagag, which has withstood both time and argument and still stands in the court.

To preserve Luxor in its historic setting and endeavour to create

Huge columns of the unfinished court of Luxor Temple.

the atmosphere and environment of ancient times, plans continue to clear the modern buildings from the two and a half kilometre ancient highway between Luxor and Karnak Temples. Meanwhile thought is being given to shifting the present gateway to the complex slightly to the north. This would enable an approach to be made, as in ancient times, through the avenue of sphinxes (some eighty of which have been excavated), towards the entrance pylon.

## DESCRIPTION

### Pylon of Ramses II

The main entrance to the temple of Luxor is by the great *Pylon of Ramses II* (Plan 2 *P.1*).[1] In front of it are six enormous statues of Ramses II, two seated and four standing. Were these statues not carved from solid granite one might imagine them to have been cast from a pair of moulds, so similar are their solid legs firmly implanted feet, square shoulders, clearcut features and eyes looking forward through all eternity.

In front of the seated figures were two pink granite obelisks. The one in position, now reinforced and repaired, has its base adorned with four praying apes on one side, and the inscriptions name Ramses II himself as the builder of this magnificent temple erected to honour Amon, blithely overlooking the fact that he was responsible only for adding to the entrance section of a temple that had stood on site for over seven hundred years. The other obelisk now stands in Paris.

The outer walls of the pylon are embellished with records of Ramses II's military campaigns, particularly against the Hittites of Syria in the fifth year of his reign. Ramses II was always anxious for his personal bravery to be recorded and his sculptors lost no time in pandering to his vanity. On the western tower (*a*) one can still make out life at the Egyptian camp (to the right) and the enthroned Pharaoh holding council (to the left). In the centre is the fortified camp with shielded soldiers and the Pharaoh himself dashing with his chariot into the fray.

The eastern tower (*b*) depicts a ferocious battle with Ramses II, still in his chariot, hurling arrows at the surrounding enemy. Dead and wounded lie beneath his feet and the enemy flee in confusion to the fortress of Kadesh from whence fresh troops appear. Kadesh itself is surrounded with battlements and the defending Hittite forces. To the extreme left, somewhat remote from the heat of the battle, the prince of the Hittites may be seen surrounded by his

---

[1] *P. 1*, etc. refers throughout to the first pylon, etc.

guards and supposedly in fear of the enemy.

## Court of Ramses II, Colonnade

Passing through the entrance pylon we enter the *Court of Ramses II* (*A*), to the left of which the Fatimide Mosque of Abu el Hagag stands in contrast to the solemn ruins of Pharonic Egypt. As recently as 1968 the local sheikhs, who claim that the tomb of the saint himself lies here, took advantage of a quiet tourist-free period, when many Egyptologists had escaped from the summer heat, to add an extension to the rear portion of the mosque, built, it will be seen, on ever weakening foundations. The height of the mosque above the stone courtyard indicates the height to which the temple was buried in sand.

The court itself is surrounded by smooth-shafted papyrus-columns with lotus-bud capitals. Standing colossi of Ramses II were placed between the first row of columns in the southern half. On each side of the doorway are a further two statues of the Pharaoh wrought in red and black granite. The one on the left has a fine statue of Queen Nefer-tari, his wife, carved near the Pharaoh's right

Statues of Ramses II, Amon and his consort Mut, Temple of Luxor.

leg. On the throne is a representation of the two Niles binding the symbols of Upper and Lower Egypt: the lotus and papyrus plants.

Adjoining the western tower of the entrance pylon (P.1) is a raised platform comprising three chambers. This was the granite shrine originally built by Hatshepsut and restored by Ramses II. The chambers were dedicated to Amon, Mut and the Moon-god Khonsu. Four papyrus columns form a colonnade on the side facing the court.

The reliefs and inscriptions which adorn the walls of the court date from the reign of Ramses II. They represent sacrifices and hymns to the gods, and all Ramses II's family, his many wives and a horde of princes and princesses are depicted on the walls.

**The Colonnade**

The *Colonnade* (B) was built by Amenhotep III. In the early morning and towards sunset heavy shadows are cast between the seven pairs of columns and the interplay of light has long been exploited by photographers as it slants from heavy architrave to calyx capitals and down the slender shafts of the columns. Though Amenhotep III conceived the idea of this colonnade. Tutankhamon, Haremhab, Seti I, Ramses II and Seti II also recorded their names there. It was Tutankhamon however who had the walls embellished with the reliefs representing the august annual festival, the *Opet*, when the god Amon visited his southern harem. The sacred barges were brought in splendid procession from Karnak to the Luxor temple, borne on the shoulders of white-robed priests from the temple to the river, and then towed upstream in a splendid and majestic procession. The festival took place at the height of the Nile flood and continued for twenty-four days of merry-making. Unhappily much of the relief work has been destroyed.

On the right-hand wall starting at (c) are preparations for the occasion, which include a rehearsal by dancing girls. The procession begins at the gate of the Karnak temple (d), which is complete with flagstaffs and from whence white-robed priests bear the sacred barge of Amon down to the water's edge. An enthusiastic audience (e) claps hands in unison and at (f) the boat in the water is being towed upstream by those on shore. A sacrifice of slaughtered animals (g) is followed by a group of acrobats, and finally offerings are made to Amon, Mut and Khonsu at the Luxor temple (h).

On the opposite wall are scenes of the return procession, including (i) sacrificial bulls being led to the scene accompanied by soldiers, standard-bearers, dancers and negro slaves who are roused

Entrance to Luxor Temple. Pylon and obelisk of Ramses II.

to frenzy by the pomp, the barges floating downstream (*j*) and the final sacrifice and offerings of flowers to Amon and Mut at the Karnak temple (*k*).

It is interesting to learn that Haremhab, the general, took advantage of the Opet to introduce himself to the populace as the next Pharaoh of Egypt at the beginning of the 19th Dynasty. Once he had been led through the streets by the priests and entered into the sacred precincts of Karnak, any question by the people as to why a man of non-royal lineage should become Pharaoh was stilled in advance. The occasion was too joyous to spoil with matters already decided by the high priests of Amon.

A fascinating cross-current in the tide of fate has led today's Muslim *Moulid*, celebrated each year during the month of *Shaaban*, closely to resemble the Opet. Muslim sheikhs emerge from the Mosque of Abu el Hagag bearing three small sailing boats which they place on carriages to traverse the city. The city is bedecked with flowers, and dancing and clapping greet the procession.

### Court of Amenhotep III
South of the colonnade is the Court of Amenhotep III (*C*), which has a double row of columns on each side and is a fine example of the architecture of Egypt's golden age. The columns are of exquisite proportion. They have clustered papyrus-bud capitals and are in a good state of repair. They were once connected by roofing blocks on the architraves leaving the court open to the sky. The doorway through which we have just passed was the entrance to the temple in Amenhotep III's reign and the sphinx-lined avenue commenced from this point.

### Hypostyle Hall
Adjoining the court to the south is the Hypostyle Hall (*D*), comprising gigantic columns arranged in four rows of eight columns each. The hall stands today as a somewhat cheerless ruin, though the walls still have reliefs of Amenhotep III before the Theban deities. The columns bear the cartouches of Ramses IV, Ramses VI, Ramses II and Seti I, mentioning the repairs carried out in their respective reigns.

To the left of the hypostyle hall stands an altar bearing Latin inscriptions dedicated to the Emperor Augustus. Adjoining the rear wall (to left and right) are two small shrines, one to Mut and one to Khonsu. The section leading off the rear originally had eight columns, which were removed when the area was converted into a

Statue of Ramses II Temple of Luxor.

Roman shrine. The doorway to the sanctuary was walled into a curved recess flanked by two granite Corinthian columns, and the exquisite 18th Dynasty reliefs were plastered over and painted with Christian themes. In places where the stucco has fallen off one can see the reliefs of Amenhotep beneath.

## Birth Room

Several small chambers surround the sanctuary, including what has become known as the Birth Room (*E*). Though in poor condition the murals are of special interest because they depict the birth of Amenhotep III.

The Egyptian Pharaoh was the embodiment of Horus, or the son of Ra or Amon. But he had, in addition, to be of direct royal lineage through his father and royal consort. If, as in the case of Amenhotep III, whose mother was not of royal Egyptian blood, his accession was not considered legitimate, he could overcome this difficulty by marrying a sister of royal lineage. Amenhotep did not do this. It was necessary for him therefore to consolidate his monarchy in other respects. Queen Hatshepsut had already shown him how. In her mortuary temple she depicted how she ruled by divine right of Amon and was, in fact, a direct descendant of the Sun-god Amon-Ra (page 82). In his temple at Luxor Amenhotep also showed that he was the son of the divine, begotten of Amon and born under the protection of the gods.

The story of the birth room is depicted in three rows on the left-hand wall (*l*). From right to left in the lower row the god Khnum moulds two infants, Amenhotep and his guardian spirit or *ka*, and fashions them on a potter's wheel. The goddess Isis sits opposite. She watches Khnum, the ram-headed god of the cataract region, playing the role of a creator god. In the next scene Amenhotep's mother is embraced by Isis in the presence of Amon. In the centre row Amon is led by the ibis-headed god of wisdom to the queen's bedchamber where he approaches her to beget the child already moulded by Khnum. The pregnancy and confinement are attended by Bes and Thoueris, the patron deities of childbirth. After the delivery Amon stands with the child in his arms in the presence of Hathor and Mut. On the much-damaged top row are the suckling of the infant king, his guardian spirits, and his presentation to Amon by Horus who promises him 'millions of years like Ra'. In the corner the grown Amenhotep stands as king.

In all other reliefs of this chamber Amenhotep is blessed by the various deities.

## Sanctuary of Alexander the Great

We now come to what has become known as the Sanctuary of
Alexander the Great (*m*), the area entirely rebuilt by him. He
removed the four original columns and placed a shrine in their stead.
Both the inner and the outer walls have reliefs representing Alexander before Amon and other deities. He obligingly left unmolested
some reliefs of Amenhotep III before various Theban deities.

In the sanctuary stood the gold-plated statue of Amon. To imbue
it with life each day the priests of Amon carried out a series of rituals.
Those carried out at dawn were the most elaborate. The statue was
first carefully cleansed. Then it was clothed with garments and
anointed with perfumes. The eyes were made up and prayers were
chanted. Then just as painstakingly the clothing and makeup were
removed and the priests humbly withdrew.

The chambers at the rear of the temple are of little significance.
One to the north has four clustered papyrus columns and three rows
of wall reliefs showing Amenhotep before Amon and other deities;
another was a sanctuary with twelve columns.

Court of Amenhotep III, Luxor Temple.

# 34

## TRADITIONALISM OF EGYPTIAN DESIGN

In order to appreciate mural design and execution it must be stressed that it was an age-old tradition, not an art form. The Egyptian painter or sculptor was not an independent or inspired creator. He was a craftsman who was part of a team which included masons, draughtsmen, jewellers and metal-workers. They all worked anonymously. Their creations were designed not for artistic appraisal nor, apart from a few exceptions, for aesthetic purposes. They formed a factory of artisans reproducing approved traditional themes with amazing accuracy. Statues for tomb or shrine were never to be seen, except by the Pharaoh or high priest, and these had a religious function. They were believed to be infused with the divine spirit of the one portrayed. Statues of the Pharaoh in open court or temple front were placed there so that the populace could gaze on the great Pharaoh who was under the protection of the gods. Praising him and praising God were one and the same thing. Amon guided the Pharaoh and the Pharaoh guided the people. This is the reason why the Egyptian monarch was repeatedly and untiringly shown in consort with the various deities. With the help of Amon, his power was absolute. The people voiced no opinions on the one hand, while he showed no weakness on the other. He was always represented in the prime of life, in powerful, confident, unbending majesty. The Pharaoh was above hopes or pleasures, fears or sufferings. In all statues and mural portrayals he was indisputably idealised and stereotyped. The torso, legs, arms and position of the head of the Pharaohs of the passing dynasties differed little. But there were subtle differences in their physiognomies. Khafre of the 4th Dynasty for example had a decidedly more prominent lower jaw than his successor Menkaure. And the lips and dents by the side of Ramses II's mouth are very different from those of Seti I, whose features are somehow finer.

It has already been noted that the distinctive characteristics of Amon, when he was not depicted as a ram with curled horns or as a man with a ram's head, were his plaited beard, his two upright plumes, his sceptre and symbol of life. The Pharaoh in turn also has characteristics: a cobra (guardian against evil) which coiled around his forehead, and a special skirt falling into a triangle in front. The decorated belt that held this in position was sometimes covered with beads or embroidery and the tail of an ox (symbol of power) was attached to it. He carried his sceptre. Etiquette was apparently carefully observed. Religious ceremonies, jubilees and other rituals, which grew more complex as time passed, conformed not only in general practice but in the most strict observance of rules and dress. Each detail has been brought down to us in the work of the relief sculptors.

Just as traditional ceremonies and rituals continued from generation to generation with very little basic change, so did the execution of mural records of the occasions become more and more stylized. The few realistic details which made their way into the representations, even as far back as the Old Kingdom, are seen repeated from dynasty to dynasty, even though they are somewhat irrelevant in terms of the symbolic and primitive purpose of the work.

Apart from the relatively short break with tradition under Akhenaten, only the efficiency and maturity of the work changed with the years. In the Luxor temple the divine immobility of the portrayals of Amenhotep III, particularly when shown in consort with the deities, are very little different from those of Ramses II some eight generations later. The same uniformity is found in the Karnak temple, which spans two thousand years.

Reconstructed head of Ramses II (in front of Luxor Temple).

# 36

## KARNAK COMPLEX    Plan 3

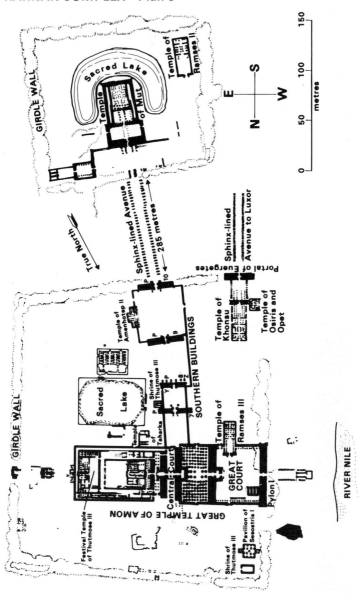

# CHAPTER 3
# THE GREAT TEMPLE OF AMON AT KARNAK

## BACKGROUND

The temple of Amon at Karnak, together with its outlying build-ings, is a natural museum of ancient Egyptian art, a blueprint of the power and glory of a golden era and a mine of historical information. Beneath its giant architraves and between bulky column and wall relief lie the records of its growth from a modest 12th Dynasty shrine to a local deity, to a temple of splendid and unimaginable proportions dedicated to the King of Gods, Amon-Ra. It owes a colonnade to one Pharaoh, a pylon to another; an inspiration here, a whim there. But each has the sole purpose of pleasing the god that would ensure them a life long, powerful and glorious.

Unravelling the secrets of two thousand years has been a major feat of Egyptology, made the more difficult by the fact that architec-tural magnificence did not necessarily run parallel with military or civic excellence. Family rivalries and kingly jealousies were as often the incentive behind a construction as creative inspiration. One cannot help being amused for example at the oft-repeated tendency of the reigning Pharaoh to alter the royal cartouche of a predecessor and so take the credit for all the work he accomplished. To add to the confusion, some parts of the buildings were raised from dis-mantled shrines or the walls of other temples. In addition, Karnak had twice to endure the degradation of Amon, at the hands of Akhenaten and of the early Christians.

An idea of the complexity of the task may be gauged when we learn that in the core of Amenhotep III's monumental third pylon were buried blocks of ten structures of earlier periods; that a valu-able historical inscription on how Kamose conquered the Hyksos —a period about which very little is known—was found text-downwards beneath a statue of Pinedjem which had been buried in the foundation of the second pylon of Ramses II; that both Ramses I and Seti I used blocks from Akhenaten's sun temple for their large-scale additions to the temple; and that Haremhab crammed his ninth pylon with thousands of inscribed sandstone blocks from this same 'heretical' era.

Thutmose I, who ascended the throne at the beginning of the 18th Dynasty, actually made the first major alterations to the original shrine. He had two colonnades and two pylons built (Plan 6 *P.4* and *P.5*). Between the latter, Hatshepsut, his daughter and builder of the magnificent mortuary temple of Deir el Bahri (page 75), erected a pair of huge obelisks. She also made some alterations to the side of the sanctuary. These were continued by her co-regent and successor Thutmose III. Though Thutmose III showed less interest in perpetuating his memory in impressive monuments than in creating an Egyptian world empire, he did build a festival temple (page 54) to the rear of the sanctuary, surrounding it with a girdle-wall, on the inner side of which were a number of small chambers.

It was Amenhotep III, builder of the temple of Luxor, who altered the front of Karnak temple. He raised a new pylon (Plan 5 *P.3*) in front of that of Thutmose I, but, impressive though it must have been, it was to be eclipsed by the additions of the 19th Dynasty. Ramses I erected the second pylon during his one year in power. Then his son, Seti I, started the construction of a huge hypostyle hall between the pylons of Ramses I and Amenhotep III. This work was continued by his successor Ramses II. Always going one better than his ancestors, Ramses II also built a second girdle-wall outside that of Thutmose III and with it the Great Temple of Amon had almost received its final, magnificent form. It was now officially and justifiably styled 'The Throne of the World'.

Seti II and Ramses III had two small separate temples built in front of the great complex. In the 22nd Dynasty under the Libyan kings of the Bubastides these were incorporated into a huge colonnaded court in front of the pylon of Ramses I. In the 25th Dynasty Taharka the Kushite also erected some gigantic columns in this court. The last addition to the temple, its entrance pylon (Plan 4 *P.1*), was erected in the Kushite Dynasty.

## DESCRIPTION

### First Pylon, Great Court, Shrine of Seti II
Seti II's two small obelisks rise on a terrace facing the Nile. From this point we approach the temple of Amon between a double row of ram-headed sphinxes. These have sun-discs on the head and a statue of the Pharaoh between the forepaws, showing the Sun-god as strong as a lion, as docile as a ram, and protective of the Pharaoh Ramses II who placed them there. We must bear in mind that in approaching the temple from the front we actually reverse, apart

from a few exceptions, the order of building.

Before us rises the massive *first pylon* (Plan 4 *P.1*) which dates from the Kushite Dynasty and which was never completed. It is 113 metres wide, 43 metres high and 5 metres thick. On the doorway leading to the Great Court is an inscription (*a*) recording the latitude and longitude of the chief temples of the Pharaohs as calculated by the group of scholars accompanying the army of Napoleon to Egypt.

The *Great Court*, which was built during the 22nd Dynasty, covers the massive area of 8,919 square metres. On the right it incorporates a small temple built by Ramses III (page 41) and on the left a small shrine built by Seti II, comprising three chambers dedicated to Amon (in the centre) and to Mut and Khonsu respectively on either side. Towards the centre of the court is the base of what was once a pair of pedestals for statues and behind this is a double colonnade. The five columns to the left are being reconstructed and the single intact column to the right is inscribed by Psemmetikh II of the 26th Dynasty, who placed his name over that of the Kushite Taharka of the 25th Dynasty. It also records the name of Ptolemy IV.

On each side of the court is a row of sphinxes. These flanked the doorway when the pylon at the rear of the court (*P.2*) formed the entrance to the temple in the reign of Ramses II. They were removed and placed near the side walls when the entrance was extended towards the Nile.

Against the inner wall of the first pylon, at (*b*), are remnants of the crude brick ramps by which the stones were heaved into position. The last two columns on this same side of the court (*c*) provide another interesting clue as to how the ancient Egyptians conducted their work. Because they were never completed they show that the roughly-shaped stones, also heaved into position on ramps, were shaped after erection and that the polishing and decoration were performed from the top downwards as the brick ramps were removed layer by layer.

The grey sandstone *Shrine of Seti II* to the left of the court was dedicated to the Karnak triad: Amon, Mut and Khonsu. The centre section, to Amon, is the best preserved. On the walls are two different representations of the deity. Near the end of the right-hand wall Amon is seated in human form with his characteristic headgear and with Mut and Khonsu seated behind him. On the left-hand wall he is depicted as a ram with the sun-disc on his head and travelling the heavens in his sacred barge. The *Holy Triad* was a common

**40**

## TEMPLE OF AMON (1)  Plan 4

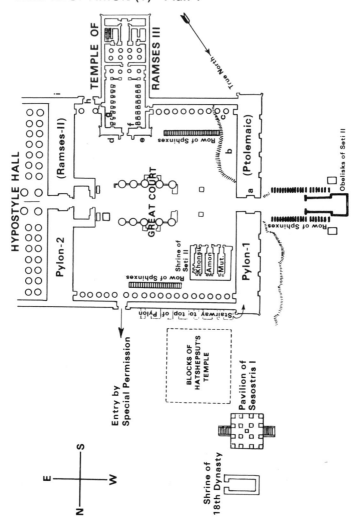

TEMPLE OF RAMSES III

HYPOSTYLE HALL

(Ramses-II)

Pylon-2

GREAT COURT

(Ptolemaic)

Pylon-1

True North

Obelisks of Seti II

Row of Sphinxes

Row of Sphinxes

Row of Sphinxes

Shrine of Seti II

Khonsu

Amon

Mut

Stairway to top of Pylon

Entry by Special Permission

BLOCKS OF HATSHEPSUT'S TEMPLE

Pavilion of Sesostris I

Shrine of 18th Dynasty

N
S
E
W

feature of the gods of ancient Egypt. At Thebes, Amon had Mut and Khonsu. At Abydos, Osiris had his sister-wife Isis and their son Horus. At Memphis, Ptah had his wife Sekhmet and their son Nefertem.

## Temple of Ramses III

Across the court stands the Temple of Ramses III. This is the only temple still standing in the whole of Egypt which was built on a homogeneous plan by a single monarch.

The pylon which forms the entrance has now been repaired and shows, on the left-hand tower (*d*), a relief of the Pharaoh wearing the double crown and holding a group of prisoners by the hair, whilst in his other hand he raises a club to smite them. Amon stands before him handing him the sword of victory and delivering to him three rows of vanquished cities each represented as a human figure rising out of a symbolic fort which bears the name of the city. On the right-hand tower (*e*) the theme is repeated but with the Pharaoh wearing the crown of Lower Egypt. Large statues of the Pharaoh flank the doorway over which Ramses III receives the symbol of life from Amon.

Passing through the entrance pylon we come to an open court surrounded by covered passages on three sides, each supported by eight square pillars with statues of Osiris in front of them. On the terrace at the rear are four similar pillars and four columns which have bud capitals. The reliefs on the back wall of the pylon (*f*) show Ramses receiving the hieroglyph for 'jubilee' from the enthroned Amon. On the east wall (*g*) is a procession of standard-bearers and the Pharaoh leading the priests who bear the sacred barges of Amon, Mut and Khonsu.

The hypostyle hall of the temple of Ramses III has eight columns with papyrus-bud capitals, adjoining which are three shrines respectively dedicated to Mut, Amon and Khonsu.

This temple is a cameo. Its charm is its size, its value is its adherence to the traditional, its historical importance is its completion according to the unadulterated blueprint of Ramses III.

Ramses III ruled at the tail end of a long line of imperial Pharaohs and he was the last of the Ramessides to carve a place for himself in history. Though wealthy—having reaped the fruits of his ancestors' battles—he was far from great, a fact that he seems himself to have recognised by placing his modest temple across the axis of the main structure at Karnak as though to say 'I do not wish to compete'. During his 32-year reign he fought three important battles, and his architectural activities included a temple at Medinet Habu (page 92) where he recorded his battles, and the initial construction of the temple of Khonsu (page 63), which was completed by his successors. He also enriched the temples of Memphis and Heliopolis but ended his days severely criticised by his contemporaries, who despised his weakened position under the priests of Amon.

### Triumphal Monument of Sheshonk I

Retracing our steps to the Great Court via the exit to the east of Ramses III's court, we find ourselves in the portico of the Bubastides (*h*) which is embellished with reliefs and inscriptions of the Pharaohs of the 22nd Dynasty. The rear door of this portico leads to the Triumphal Monument of Sheshonk I, which is situated on the outside of the southern tower of the second pylon (*i*). This scene commemorates the victory of Shishak of the Bible over Rehoboam, son of Solomon the King of Judah, when Solomon's temple was robbed of its riches. Beneath Amon is the goddess Mut holding a club, bow and quiver, leading five rows of captives carved in perfect symmetry. To the right Sheshonk is grasping a group of captives by the hair and striking them with his raised club. The Biblical passages covering this campaign are:

'*And it came to pass in the fifth year of king Rehoboam, that Shishak king of Egypt came up against Jerusalem: and he took away the treasures of the house of the Lord, and the treasures of the king's house; he even took away all: and he took away all the shields of gold which Solomon had made.*' (*1 Kings 14:25–6*)

' *... And it came to pass, that in the fifth year of king Rehoboam, Shishak king of Egypt came up against Jerusalem, because they had transgressed against the Lord, with twelve hundred chariots, and threescore thousand horsemen: and the people were without number that came with him out of Egypt ...*' (*2nd Chro. 12:2–3*)

### Second Pylon, Great Hypostyle Hall

We return to the great court of the temple and proceed towards the *second pylon*, the pylon of Ramses II (*P.2*). The centre section was originally restored by the Ptolemies. It is now being reconstructed after the removal of the blocks from Akhenaten's Sun Temples to Aten which were used as filling for the core. Just before the pylon is a small vestibule flanked by two large statues. The one on the left, in red granite, is of Ramses II, later usurped by Pinedjem. This is the statue already mentioned (page 37) as having been found under

The statue usurped by Pinedjem, son-in-law of the high priest.

the second pylon.

The *Great Hypostyle Hall*, fruit of Egypt's power and wealth and one of the most massive of human creations, covers an area of 4,983 square metres. To support the roof 134 columns were arranged in sixteen rows. The double row of central columns leading from the doorway of the second pylon eastwards towards the sanctuary is higher than the others. The smooth-shafted central columns are twenty-one metres high and are topped with calyx capitals large enough to hold one hundred standing men. The somewhat squat side columns have bud capitals and the discrepancy in height is made up by square pillars between the steps of the roof. The space between these pillars once held windows and served to light the entire hall, revealing that the walls, the shafts of the columns, the architrave and in fact every available space was covered with inscriptions and reliefs. It has been stated in almost every description of this hall to date, but must nevertheless be repeated here, that the whole of the cathedral of Notre Dame in Paris could be comfortably accommodated within its walls.

**TEMPLE OF AMON   Plan 5**

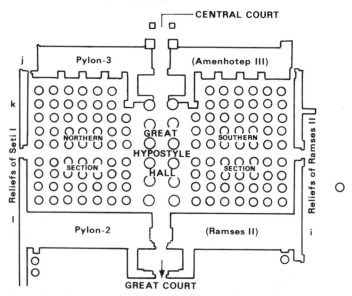

The hypostyle hall was planned and begun by Ramses I and was continued by his son Seti I on a scale far surpassing Amenhotep III's unfinished hypostyle hall at Luxor. It was finally completed by Seti's son Ramses II. Although Seti I was responsible for the construction of the entire northern half of the hall and also the central aisle, and although Ramses II built only the southern portion, it is the latter who has secured credit for the greater part of the work.

The overall effect is awe-inspiring. Although some critics have commented on the less-than-elegant columns at the sides or on the fact that 'you can't see the trees for forest', its magnificence is indisputable. When Napoleon's learned entourage first saw it, the hall looked as though devastated by a hurricane. Leaning columns seemed on the verge of collapse, many were already prostrate and the flag-stones were littered with debris. French Egyptologists working for the Department of Antiquities devoted their energies to reconstruction. The work of Georges Legrain, followed by Maurice Pillet and finally Henri Chevrier, who completed a 25-year mission as Director of Works at Karnak in 1956, left the Great Hypostyle Hall erect and proud.

The 'forest' of side columns of the Hypostyle Hall, Karnak Temple.

# 46

Only one single column (the first in the sixth row) bears the name of Ramses I, who started its construction in his brief two year reign. It may be noticed that the reliefs of Seti I (in the northern portion) are in flat relief and are somewhat more delicate than the deeper, more definite inscriptions of Ramses II (in the southern portion from the eleventh row). Most of the reliefs depict adoration of the Theban god. Ramses III, Ramses IV, Ramses VI and Ramses XII all recorded their names.

On the outside of the hypostyle hall are some important historical reliefs. These are accessible from the exit at the side or from the central court. They are portrayals of Seti I's and Ramses II's military campaigns in Asia, the like of which had not been seen for two generations since the expansion of the empire under Thutmose III. There are over sixty metres of representations from the spectacular charges into the foe with arrows and chariots to the ultimate presentation of prisoners of war to Amon, Mut and Khonsu.

Ramses II's campaign was against the Hittites. It is depicted on the southern wall and contains the actual text of the treaty, the earliest surviving international non-aggression pact. According to the treaty each state, having equal, independent status, renounced all ideas of aggression against the other. It declared that peace should henceforth prevail between the two kings and all their dependents and reaffirmed earlier treaties existing between the two countries. A mutual defence alliance, co-operation in the humane treatment of disloyal subjects and also in the extradition of political refugees and immigrants, formed clauses of the pact.

It bore the title:

*'The treaty which the great chief of Kheta, Khetasar, the valiant, the son of Merasar, the great chief of Kheta, the valiant, the grandson of Seplel, the great chief of Kheta, the valiant, made, upon a silver tablet for Usermare-Setepnere (Ramses II), the great ruler of Egypt, the valiant, the son of Seti I, the great ruler of Egypt, the valiant; the grandson of Ramses I, the great ruler of Egypt, the valiant; the good treaty of peace and of brotherhood, setting peace between them forever.'*[1]

Witnesses to the treaty were a thousand gods and goddesses of the land of the Hittites and a thousand gods and goddesses from the land of Egypt.

The battle scenes are similar to those on the first pylon of the temple of Luxor already described (pages 26/27).

Seti I's battles took place in Lebanon, southern Palestine, and Syria, and are depicted on the northern wall. The series begins on the eastern wall (Plan 5*j*) where (in the upper row) Seti alights from

---

[1] James Breasted, *A History of Egypt*, Hodder and Stoughton, 1950, pp. 437/438. In Hittite, Khetasur is Khattishili III, Merasar is Murshili II, Seplal is Shuppiluilumas.

his chariot in the wooded Lebanon. The Lebanese are obliged to cut down trees for the Pharaoh. In the lower row Seti is in battle with the bedouins of southern Palestine (to the right). He drives his chariot, drawn by two horses, whilst firing arrows at the enemy. Confused heaps of dead and wounded lie on the ground. The fortress of Canaan, above the battlefield, is used as a hideout and the inhabitants assist fugitives to escape into it.

On the left-hand section of the main wall (*k*) is the battle in Syria. In the upper row the Pharaoh advances to the front line of the attack, shooting arrows that send the enemy, both charioteers and cavalry, fleeing in confusion. In the fortress which is surrounded by a moat the inhabitants are surprisingly carved full face as they peer from behind trees. Seti is also depicted binding captives, leading or dragging them. Two rows of captured Syrians are presented to Amon, Mut and Khonsu along with valuable booty.

In the lower row is a triumphal march through Palestine (left), a battle with the bedouins of southern Palestine and (right) the victorious march from Syria. The border between Asia and Africa is marked by a crocodile-infested canal bordered by reeds and linked

The Hypostyle Hall, Karnak Temple. Calyx capitals of the central columns.

# 48

by a bridge. At each end of this bridge is a fortified guardhouse and, on the home front, Seti is welcomed by groups of priests carrying garlanded flowers. Captives and booty are presented to Amon.

On the right-hand wall (*l*) is the battle of Kadesh (in the top row), the battle against the Libyans (in the middle row), and the battle against the Hittites in northern Syria (in the lower row). The defenders of Kadesh are pierced by arrows. The Libyans, distinguished by a single plaited braid and feathers, are smitten with the sword. The Hittites, shot at by the charioted Pharaoh, take flight on foot, on horseback and in chariot. In the lower row, when Seti hands his captives and the captured vessels over to Amon, Mut and Khonsu, the goddess of truth is present.

On each side of the doorway separating these two walls (*k* and *l*) are colossal representations of Amon holding several rows of captured nations and cities by cords and presenting the sword of victory to Seti I. Seti raises his club against a band of foes whom he dangles by the hair.

### Third Pylon, Pavilion of Sesostris I, Central Court

At the rear of the hypostyle hall is the reconstructed *third pylon* (*P.3*) built by Amenhotep III. It certainly needs more than a little imagination to reconstruct in the mind's eye the gold and silver inlay, the flagstaffs and splendour of this one-time entrance to the temple. When Amenhotep III was constructing it he was simultaneously finalising plans for the colonnaded hall at the Luxor temple. Together they formed his most impressive architectural achievements.

Some years ago when soil drainage was being checked to avoid the crumbling of columns from undermining, the pylon was found to contain in its core the ruins of temples and shrines of earlier periods. The task of extracting the inscribed or painted blocks deep in the pylon's foundation, whilst propping up existing walls prior to reconstruction, was, and still is, an exacting one. And the matching of the extracted pieces with their partners in pattern and history has been extremely time-consuming. But with the successful removal and complete reconstruction of some of the lost masterpieces, these labours have received their supreme reward.

The *Pavilion of Sesostris I*, a 12th Dynasty structure erected for the Jubilee of the Pharaoh, is the earliest structure at Karnak today. Its blocks were rescued from obscurity and reassembled just north of the main temple to Amon within the girdle-wall, where it can be seen by special permission. The walls of the pavilion are made of fine limestone, and the reliefs, minutely and precisely carved in high relief, are amongst the finest to be found in Luxor. They show the restraint and austerity typical of the Middle Kingdom when the work was unencumbered by too much detail. The simple shrine consists of sixteen square pillars and the pedestal on which the Amon barge was placed to let the priestly bearers rest. It has been decided that the original site was on one side of the paved thoroughfare leading from Karnak temple to Luxor temple.

The earliest structure at Karnak: 12th Dynasty Pavilion of Sesostris I.

A shrine which can be traced to the reigns of Amenhotep I and Thutmose I was also found in the foundations of the third pylon and has been reconstructed immediately to the north of the Pavilion of Sesostris. It is made of alabaster. Since this was a medium used mainly for statues and offering-tables it is not often that we find a shrine or temple in alabaster. It is small, simple, of beautiful proportions and in nearly perfect condition. On the right-hand of the inner wall is a particularly lovely representation of the Pharaoh kneeling before a table of offerings.

Also extracted from Amenhotep's third pylon are finely inscribed granite blocks that must once have been a dramatic structure in red and black, built by Queen Hatshepsut. Her figure, carved in low relief, has not been defaced.

One cannot help wondering why temples and shrines were dismantled and used for new constructions. Akhenaten's temple to Aten is easily explained because with his passing the worship of Amon was reinstated and reference to sun-worship was obliterated. But why should the exquisite temple of Sesostris have been hidden in a pylon? And the temple of Hatshepsut? Because she was a woman and not recognised as a Pharaoh of Egypt, despite her beard, male dress and attempts to prove her divine origin? Then why should the small and exquisite alabaster shrine have been destined for the same fate? The illustrious Amenhotep the Magnificent could hardly have been short of raw material.

Only one thing is certain: but for the continuous efforts of Egyptologists, particularly in the last sixty years, many if not all of these hidden wonders would have been lost forever.

In the *Central Court* of the temple is the last survivor of four obelisks erected by Thutmose I and III, the former under the faithful guidance of his chief architect, Ineni, who brought them from the granite quarries of Aswan. There are three vertical inscriptions on each face of this obelisk: the central one dedicated by Thutmose I himself, the other two additions by Ramses IV and VI.

### Fourth, Fifth and Sixth Pylons

We now proceed to a much ruined part of the temple. The *fourth pylon* (*P.4*), built by Thutmose I, is followed by a *colonnade* with a strange and interesting history. Within this enclosed area are clues to family feuds, petty jealousies and religious differences, to say nothing of Pharonic vanity. The colonnade was originally designed by Thutmose I and it was planned to have a roof of cedar. In it stands an obelisk (Plan 6 *m*). This lofty spire was one of two erected by Queen Hatshepsut, who removed part of the roof of her father's colonnade to place them there. Hatshepsut's co-regent and successor, Thutmose III, at a later date in the family feud had a wall built to hide the obelisks of his predecessor, this being a simpler expedient than their removal and destruction. The wall covered most of the obelisk, masking it from people within the temple. The figure of Amon was obliterated by Akhenaten and restored by Seti I, thus putting an end to the vicissitudes suffered for two hundred years by the colonnade of Thutmose I.

The beautiful towering obelisk of Hatshepsut was erected in the 16th year of her reign. It was made of a single block of pink Aswan granite of the finest quality. The apex was once covered with a mixture of gold and silver. This lofty spire records the fact that it was made in seven months. It weighs something like 317,515 kilogrammes (700,000 lbs). One cannot but marvel at the tenacity required merely to quarry it, let alone to cart it to the Nile, transport it along its waters, disembark it and finally erect it with perfect accuracy on a pedestal.

## TEMPLE OF AMON   Plan 6

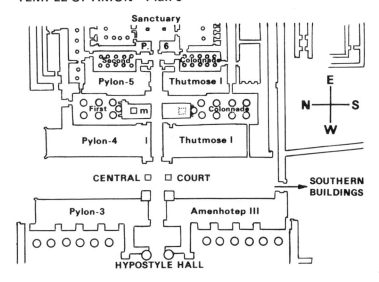

# 52

Forming the rear wall of the colonnade is the *fifth pylon* (*P.5*), also erected by Thutmose I. Passing through it we enter Thutmose I's second colonnade, which originally comprised twenty sixteen-sided columns. It is now very much in ruin. On each side of the central passage Thutmose III constructed a pair of chambers and beyond this rises the last and smallest pylon, the *sixth pylon* (Plan 7 *P.6*) erected by Thutmose III. On each face of the pylon (*n*) are lists of tribes of the south which were subjugated by Thutmose III's army, and also those of Syria, which alone number 119. The conquered territories are shown as an elliptical hieroglyph character surmounted by a human bust with arms bound behind the back. The Syrians are depicted with pointed beards and heavy robes. In long processions they bear their tributes to be recorded by the vizier.

## Hall of Records, Sanctuary
The granite gateway of the sixth pylon was restored by Seti I and as we pass through it we enter what has become known as the *Hall*

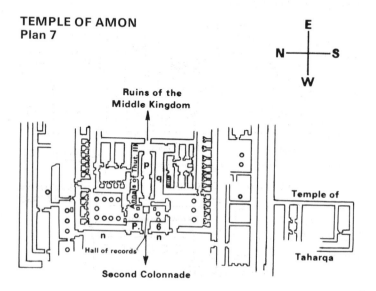

**TEMPLE OF AMON**
**Plan 7**

*of Records* of Thutmose III. These were the state records made by the priests of the temple to detail the sources of gifts and booty received by them. Of course, following Thutmose's military victories, Karnak was now increasingly filled with gold and silver treasures from far afield, as well as with magnificent bronze weapons of war and furniture of ivory and ebony.

The most characteristic feature of this Hall of Records are the two stately granite pillars (*o*), one bearing the lotus of Upper Egypt and the other the papyrus of Lower Egypt in high relief. These rather unusual twin symbols emphasise that the unity of the two lands, formed and broken many times in their long history, was intact in the 18th Dynasty.

Beyond is the *Sanctuary* (*p*) comprising two chambers. It is of pink granite and was constructed by the half-brother of Alexander the Great, Philip Arrhidaeus, on the site of an earlier chamber. The walls are finely carved and coloured; the reliefs on the upper reaches

Crowning ceremony of Philip Arrhidaeus (upper row). Priests bearing sacred barges of Amon (lower row): Sanctuary, Karnak Temple.

of the wall still retain their colour. On the outer wall of the sanctuary on the right-hand side (*q*) is a superb relief in excellent condition of Philip being crowned and presented to the gods (above) and of the festal barges of Amon being carried in priestly procession (below). On the left-hand outer wall of the sanctuary are the *Annals of Thutmose III*, depicting details of the cities and tribes subdued in his military campaigns.

Leaving the sanctuary we come to a large open space where there are very scanty remains of Middle Kingdom structures. Beyond rises the Great Festival Temple of Thutmose III.

## Great Festival Temple of Thutmose III: Plan 8

Before describing this 'Most Glorious of Monuments' as it was called, let us first recall that Thutmose III was the creator of a vast Egyptian empire. He went regularly to war each summer and returned to Egypt around the end of September. Among the splendid treasures he brought back with him were golden vases, arms and armour, precious metals and countless jewels. During the balmy winter months he would remain in Egypt where he would receive foreign envoys; sometimes these were members of the royal or noble classes, and sometimes representatives accompanied by caravans of costly gifts. Then, when the summer sun shone hot and dry, he would recruit his forces and march to battle once again. In a series of annals he gave full details of his seventeen campaigns and records of the spoils of battle. He was the first Egyptian Pharaoh to introduce military tactics, his most successful battle technique being the *blitzkrieg*: some 3,000 chariots, hidden behind a hill, simultaneously dashing into action with lances flying, hooves whipping up the dust, soldiers yelling. The resulting confusion in the enemy ranks was designed to weaken their morale. It inevitably did.

Thutmose III was no war-monger. He never appointed Egyptian governors over the conquered territories. Instead he gave power to the local chieftains and, moreover, started cultural relations by bringing the sons of the chieftains to Egypt to study and absorb Egyptian culture, ideology and religion before returning to their homelands.

Following the victories of Thutmose III Egypt was justifiably imbued with a feeling of national pride, while the victor himself humbly gave thanks to Amon to the rear of the national temple at Karnak.

The *Festival Temple of Thutmose III* is spacious and elegant, 44 metres wide and 16 deep. The roof is supported by 20 columns in two rows and 32 square pillars on the sides. One immediately notices a lack of conformity; Thutmose ordered his workers to taper the columns downwards and not upwards and to top them with peculiar inverted calyx capitals. The capital gives a sort of tent-like effect and may have been designed to assuage the Pharaoh's thirst for outdoor living. It was never repeated. The effect is definitely clumsy. The reliefs on the pillars, which are shorter than the columns, show Thutmose III in the presence of the gods.

Grouped around the sanctuary, which comprises three chambers, were some fifty small halls and chambers. Most lie in ruin today. To the left of the sanctuary is a chamber with four clustered papyrus columns (*r*). The lower parts of the walls are decorated with exotic

**TEMPLE OF AMON    Plan 8**

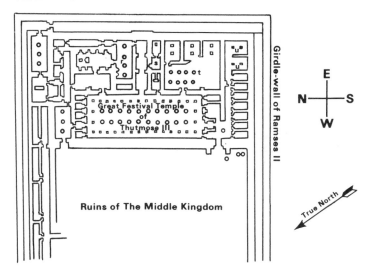

plants and animals brought to Egypt from Syria in the 25th year of the Pharaoh's reign. It says a great deal for the character of Thutmose III that, despite his prowess as a warrior, his ability to topple the powerful Queen Hatshepsut from the throne and his vow to revenge his people for their conquest by the Hyksos, he should have found time and interest to import flowers and animals into his native land.

To the right of the sanctuary is what is now known as the *Alexander Room* (*s*). It was originally built by Thutmose III and was restored by Alexander the Great. The reliefs show Alexander, and in some instances Thutmose III, sacrificing to the gods.

To the south of the Alexander Room is a hall with eight sixteen-sided columns (*t*). The two small chambers with columns (*u*), followed by seven other chambers, carry reliefs of Thutmose III.

### Rear Section of Temple of Amon, Sacred Lake
Plan 3 will show that the entire portion eastwards from the fifth pylon, or in other words the rear section of the temple of Karnak, was surrounded by a girdle-wall. What remains of this is embellished with reliefs of Ramses II sacrificing to the various deities. His colonnade at the far end just outside this girdle-wall is now a jumble of ruins and beyond this is a small temple also built by him, and an ancient gateway which dates from the time of the Ptolemies.

To the south of this section of Karnak is the *Sacred Lake*, the symbol of Nun the eternal ocean, where the priests of Amon purified themselves in the holy water. Unfortunately too few of the hewn rocks survived the years to allow of genuine restoration. The gigantic stone beetle or *scarab* that overlooks the lake was one of four placed there by Amenhotep III in honour of the Sun-god.

### Southern Buildings, Karnak Cachette, Seventh to Tenth Pylons
The buildings extending southwards from the central court of the main temple of Karnak are mostly in ruin today. A brief survey will be made, however, to show the importance of the plan of reconstruction over the next ten years. A group of French architects are under contract with the Department of Antiquities for the complete reconstruction of the Karnak area, of which this is only one section, but perhaps the most important.

Proceeding from the central court (lying between the third and fourth pylons) are the remains of a court where there is a good view of Ramses II's famous treaty with the Hittites, mentioned on pages

Granite pillars bearing the symbols of Upper and Lower Egypt, Hall of Records, Karnak Temple.

## KARNAK TEMPLE—Southern Buildings

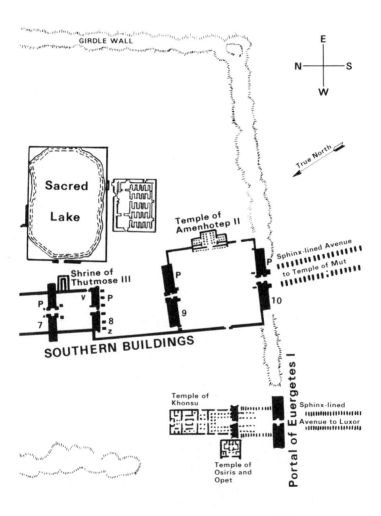

GIRDLE WALL

E
N — S
W

True North

Sacred Lake

Temple of Amenhotep II

Sphinx-lined Avenue to Temple of Mut

Shrine of Thutmose III

P        v        P

P.        P
7        8
z

9

10

P

SOUTHERN BUILDINGS

Portal of Euergetes I

Temple of Khonsu

Sphinx-lined Avenue to Luxor

Temple of Osiris and Opet

46/47, followed by the seventh pylon (*P.7*). This court was the site of a temple of the Middle Kingdom and it was here that Legrain extracted a fantastic number of works of art from what became known as the *Karnak Cachette*. Buried in a pit were thousands of pieces including statues in stone and bronze, sphinxes and sacred animals. The bronze items alone numbered 17,000. It seems that one of the Pharaohs decided to have a spring clean in the temple and remove all the junk. Though most of the pieces are of little artistic merit, the find shows that the temple could well have housed the 86,486 statues mentioned in the Great Harris Papyrus.

The *seventh pylon* (*P.7*) was built by Thutmose III, and facing it to the south are the remains of two colossal statues of him in red granite. Between the walls uniting the seventh and eighth pylons, to the east, is a small shrine dating also from the reign of Thutmose III.

The *eighth pylon* (*P.8*) was the work of Queen Hatshepsut and is the most ancient part of the structure. In fact there is very little proof of her having built this pylon, for her name was removed from the reliefs by Thutmose II. And following Akhenaten's removal of

Reconstructed statues by the Eighth Pylon, Karnak Temple.

all allusions to Amon, Seti I restored them, often inserting his own name in place of those of the older rulers. Reconstruction of this area may yet supply the missing clues to the overlapping reigns of the Thutmosides.

In the doorway at the rear left-hand of this court (Plan 3 *v*) is an important historical relief on the left. It is the first instance in Egypt's long history where the high priest, in this case Amenhotep, is depicted in the same size as the Pharaoh. Standing with arms uplifted, Amenhotep offers flowers to Ramses IX. This relief indicates the growth of priestly power. Faithful traditionalists of the established religion, the priests of Amon had hitherto been righteous, just and devout. The power of leadership had been firmly vested in the throne and they had recognised and accepted this. Over the years however their simple piety had turned to mild interest in earthly matters, then acute interest, and finally to intrigue and a craving for political power. The high priest depicted in this mural makes offerings to the Pharaoh while being draped in linen by two servants. A reciprocal gesture of appreciation? Or a royal bribe?

Beyond the eighth pylon is a row of six royal personages. The best preserved are Amenhotep I (in limestone) and Thutmose II (in red granite) both to the west.

The *ninth pylon* (*P.9*) was built by Haremhab the one-time general. When repairs started it was found to be filled, like its companion the *tenth pylon* (*P.10*), with blocks from Akhenaten's Temple to the Sun. Together with the 40,000–odd blocks from this same period found beneath the hypostyle hall and the second pylon, these number some 60,000 blocks and are valuable clues to a period about which there are many gaps in our knowledge. When the first small, distinctively uniform sandstone blocks were discovered in the pylon of Ramses II, it was at first erroneously assumed that they had been brought up-river from a dismantled temple in Tel el Amarna. Drainage operations subsequently led to the excavation of parts of no less than seventeen colossal statues of Akhenaten himself. Akhenaten in fact had sun temples erected before he changed his capital to Tel el Amarna and while Thebes was witnessing the slow introduction of a new religious concept.

## Akhenaten's Sun Temples at Karnak
The first scientific study of antiquities by computer was started in 1966 by the University Museum of Pennsylvania, subsidised in part by the Egyptian Antiquities Department and in part by the Smith-

Statue of Amenhotep II in Karnak Temple.

sonian Institution. It entailed a systematic study of the distinctive sandstone blocks, called *Talatat*, found at different sites at Karnak this century, but particularly from the 9th pylon of Haremhab. Painstaking work with scale photographs enabled the matching of decorations and representations into chains of scenes, from which it soon became clear that there was not one, but as many as half a dozen different Sun Temples.

In the 1975/76 archeological season the site of one of the temples was found. Donald Redford, Director of the Archeological team for the University of Pennsylvania, excavating an area east of Karnak, located the foundations of a long wall, together with fragments of relief which identify it as the Temple of Gem-pa-Aten (see Work in Progress No. 12).

Meanwhile, the Franco-Egyptian Centre at Karnak continue to extract *Talatat* from the core of the 9th pylon. The blocks were buried in the order in which the temple was dismantled; this enables immediate reconstruction and, in fact, an 18-metre wall has been reconstructed in the Luxor Museum (page 180).

The eastern avenue of sphinxes extends from the tenth pylon to the Gate of Philadelphus, which is excellently preserved. The temple of Mut is to the south. To the west is the temple of Khonsu and the temple of Osiris adjoins it.

## TEMPLE OF KHONSU    Plan 9

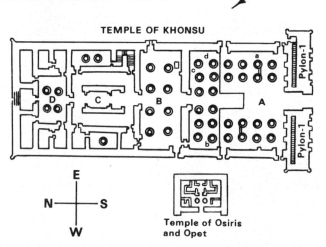

**Temple of Osiris and Opet**

## Temple of Khonsu: Plan 9

The Temple of Khonsu, dedicated to the Moon-god Khonsu, son of Amon and Mut, is a classical example of a New Kingdom temple. Ramses III was responsible for building the original sanctuary and erecting the walls but it was only completed under his successors Ramses IV, who continued the near chambers and added a small hypostyle hall, Ramses XII, and Hrihor, the high priest who seized the throne at the close of the 20th Dynasty. Hrihor added a colonnaded court and the entrance pylon. In the 21st Dynasty the temple was continued under Pinedjem I.

The large pylon at the entrance (Plan 9 *P.1*) has representations of the high priest and his wife making sacrifices to various Theban deities. The high priest, Hrihor, stands in the position traditionally occupied by the Pharaohs of Egypt. The four vertical grooves with corresponding apertures in the masonry at the front of the pylon were used to fasten the flagstaffs.

Passing through the central portal of the pylon, decorated with

Thutmose III in a traditional scene showing the punishment of all enemy countries.

reliefs of Alexander II, we enter the Court (*A*). This has four side-exits and is surrounded on three sides by colonnades of papyrus columns with bud capitals formed in double rows. Those at the rear of the court are on a raised terrace.

There is a representation on the right-hand wall (*a*) showing the main pylon of the temple with eight, not four, flagstaffs. On the walls of the terrace Hrihor makes offerings to Amon, Mut and Khonsu (*b*). At (*c*) he receives gifts from Khonsu and there are also representations of the sacred barge. At (*d*) Hrihor offers flowers to an image of Min, the god of human fertility.

Through the doorway at the back of the court is the hypostyle hall (*B*) which spans the full breadth of the temple. The four papyrus columns in the central aisle have calyx capitals whilst the smaller side ones have bud capitals. The wall reliefs were added by Ramses XII and depict him sacrificing to the gods in the presence of Hrihor, who later dethroned him.

The central doorway in the rear wall leads to the sanctuary (*C*). The reliefs represent the Pharaohs Ramses IV, Ramses XII and various deities.

Behind the sanctuary, on each side of which are small chambers with reliefs of Ramses IV, is a small door of the Ptolemaic period leading to a small hall (*D*) which has four twenty-sided columns. The reliefs mostly depict Ramses IV but there are also some representations of the Emperor Augustus on each side of the entrance. There are seven small chambers, decorated by Ramses III and his successors, surrounding this hall.

The temple of Khonsu is of special historical significance since it bears witness to the transmission of Pharonic power, between the reigns of Ramses III and Ramses XII, from the royal line of Pharaohs to the priests of Amon. As already mentioned the high priests gradually acquired more political power after the close of the 18th Dynasty. With an ever-weakening line of Pharaohs after Ramses II they were at last able to usurp the throne. In this temple the name of the high priest appears in a royal cartouche for the first time.

## Temple of Osiris and Opet: Plan 9

The Temple of Osiris and Opet adjoins that of Khonsu to the south-west. It comprises a rectangular hall which has a well-preserved ceiling resting on two Hathor-decorated columns, a second small hall which is flanked by two rooms, and a sanctuary. The sanctuary has representations of King Euergetes II before various deities.

A flight of steps from the sanctuary leads to the lower chambers of the basement and the exit door, which once connected this temple with that of Khonsu.

## Temple of Mut

Now completely in ruins, the Temple of Mut was surrounded on three sides by a horseshoe-shaped lake. It was dedicated to the consort of Amon and comprised a pair of open courts, one following the other, and a sanctuary surrounded by ante-chambers. The construction extended through many generations from Amenhotep III to Ptolemaic times.

Among its many statues and murals is a grotesque figure of the god Bes, and at least 600 statues of the war-goddess Sekhmet in black granite. These surrounded the entire court, in places packed closely in double rows. We know very little about the beginning of the adoration of the goddess in whose honour this temple was built, and the site is covered with centuries of rubble. It is now, at long last, being excavated by a team from the Brooklyn Museum in New York. (see Work in Progress No. 3).

Amenhotep II was known for his enormous muscular strength. His arrows pierce a sheet of Asian copper. (Luxor Museum)

## CHAPTER 4  THE NECROPOLIS
## INTRODUCTION

It was to the West, where the Sun-god at the end of each day began his nocturnal journey through the underworld, that man also gained admittance to the hereafter. Life after death was a concept most deeply rooted in the minds of the ancient Egyptians. Since the earliest times they had seen the passing of the mortal body not as an end but as a beginning. Belief in the hereafter was the focal point of their outlook. It stimulated their thought, their moral principles and their art.

Man, as they saw him, comprised the body, the spirit (or *ba*), and the *ka*, a sort of guardian double which, though born at the same time, did not share death with him. After the passing of his mortal body man could live again through his *ka*, provided that it was nourished and surrounded by all that was necessary for a continued existence. His *ba* or spirit ascended to higher spheres and could fly around the world and return to the tomb, provided that his body was properly preserved. Without the body, in fact, there could be no continued existence. So it can readily be seen that the repository for the dead and the manner in which they were to be interred were of the utmost importance.

Even in pre-dynastic times the dead, laid to rest in simple oval pits surmounted by a pile of rubble, were covered with a protective animal skin and surrounded by pots containing food and drink, a few primitive weapons and ornaments. Each slow development from these crude pit burials through the *mastaba* development to the pyramid proper, and its ultimate abandonment in favour of rock-hewn tombs, was a battle to preserve the body. When a stone super-structure was placed atop a tomb in place of the rubble, this was because it was a stronger safeguard against the elements. When, in place of skin, linen cloth was used to swathe the body, this was because it afforded better protection. When the tombs were made deeper, when a system of blocking entrance passages was devised, when funerary customs underwent change, each stage was an advancement in the protection of the body to allow the deceased to live again, for ever.

*Mastabas*, low rectangular bench-like brick structures, were tombs. The earliest comprised a single burial chamber hewn deep in the ground, in which the deceased, placed in a wooden sarcophagus, lay surrounded by pottery jars filled with food, drink and ointments, and chests of weapons and jewellery. In the funerary room built in the superstructure there was a false door through which the *ka* could join the world of the living. In front of it was an offering table where relatives and friends could place food and drink to sustain the deceased in the hereafter.

Since tombs were regarded as the places where the deceased would dwell, they closely resembled contemporary houses both inside and out. Naturally, increased prosperity meant a better life and, since a man's good fortune led to an increased concern to take it all with him to the hereafter, the *mastaba* underwent transformation. It became larger and more complex, constructed to fit each individual's special requirements. The sarcophagus, still laid in the central chamber of the substructure, stood on a platform. Other chambers were constructed for the funerary equipment. Abundant food and drink meant more sustenance for the body. Perfected furniture meant more eternal comfort. Ointments, weapons, games, clothing, all meant a better after-life. And since it was desirable to be surrounded by loved ones, chambers were sometimes constructed for the wife, sons and daughters of the deceased.

But larger tombs and richer funerary equipment led to increased risk of violation by robbers. It is somewhat ironical that, whereas mummification was to be perfected and art and architecture were to rise to a high degree of sophistication, no secure method of hindering the robber was ever found. During fifty centuries tombs were violated, their contents taken and the bodies exposed to the elements.

The burial chamber and adjoining rooms for the funerary equipment were originally constructed first and then, after the superstructure was raised, the deceased and his belongings were lowered through the roof of the *mastaba*, down the pit and straight into the burial chamber. With bigger and more elaborate tombs, however, an easier means of entry had to be devised. Access was thenceforth made via a stairway from a point outside the superstructure and leading directly underground to the tomb chamber. It was hoped that robbers would be deterred by an elaborate system of blockings.

In many *mastabas* dating from the latter part of the 4th Dynasty a special room was constructed in the superstructure, separated by a wall from the other rooms. This was the *statue house*, now known by the Arabic name of *serdab* or cellar, where a statue or statues of the tomb's owner were placed. It was considered as the seat for his *ka* and there were slits in the intervening wall which enabled the *ka* to see the light of day, watch the offering ceremonies and enjoy the scent of the burning incense. The slits themselves were known as *the eyes of the ka-house*. In this way the deceased, lying underground in his tomb chamber, had his *ka* supervising the offering ceremonies on his behalf. But how could he be sure that future generations of his relatives would continue to bring him food and drink? To ensure continued nourishment he had himself represented on the tomb walls in the act of receiving sacrificial offerings. These representations of food and drink were believed to serve him in place of the real thing. Not surprisingly this was only one step away from believing that anything depicted on the walls of a tomb was as good as the real thing: a well-stocked farmyard, healthy cattle, a large house and garden, numerous servants.

Royal tombs were originally large brick *mastabas*. In fact the Step Pyramid of Sakkara, the first stone building in history, started as a *mastaba* and grew to its characteristic proportions as a result of successive additions. Thenceforth the tombs of the head of state steadily surpassed the tombs of the people in size and magnificence. In time the steps were filled in and the outer casing was made smooth until the full pyramid form developed. These vast stone structures, designed in geometrical simplicity, represent a great technical achievement. To the east of each pyramid was a mortuary temple where a priesthood conducted rituals and maintained the tomb complex. A covered causeway connected it with a valley temple which stood at the foot of the plateau.

The pyramids, of which the great 4th Dynasty Pyramid of Khufu (Cheops) at Giza is the most famous, failed to safeguard the bodies of the Pharaohs. Though some of these vast structures stand as imperishable landmarks, they were probably robbed as early as the uncertain period following the fall of the monarchy at Memphis in the 6th Dynasty. Yet, surprisingly, for over six centuries, until Thutmose I came to the throne in the 18th Dynasty, the pyramid continued to be the tomb constructed for the royalty of Egypt.

Amenhotep I was the first Pharaoh to break with the ancient custom. He saw that the durable pyramids had failed to safeguard the bodies of his ancestors, that blind alleys and hidden chambers never fooled a robber. Now he attempted secrecy to give him the eternal security he craved. For his tomb he chose a site high on the hills south of the Valley of the Kings and built his mortuary temple in the valley. His successor, Thutmose I, followed his innovation of separating the burial chamber from the mortuary temple, being the first Pharaoh to contruct his tomb in the Valley of the Kings. His architect Ineni excavated it through solid rock across a precipitous valley, and recorded for posterity on a stele in his tomb that he carried out his Pharaoh's request 'no one seeing and no one hearing'. His mortuary temple was built at the edge of the verdant valley on the west bank of the Nile. Thus, he believed, could his cult be continued while his actual resting place was unknown.

This precedent was followed. The Pharaohs that succeeded Thutmose I in the 18th, 19th and 20th Dynasties continued to dig their tombs deep in the sterile valley which is now known as the *Valley of the Kings*. Royal consorts and children from the 19th Dynasty were buried at a separate site, the *Valley of the Queens*. Noblemen had their tombs dug at various cemeteries among the foothills of the range.

El Fadlya Canal runs parallel with the Nile, at Luxor.

# 70

This is the Theban necropolis, the *City of the Dead*. It was not always as lifeless as we see it today. At one time beside each mortuary temple there were dwellings for the priests and stables for the sacrificial animals. Nearby were the guardhouses and granaries each with its superintendent. Surrounding or in front of each temple were lakes, groves and beautifully laid-out gardens.

Beside the mortuary temples there were also large palaces where the pharaohs took up temporary residence, to supervise the progress on their monuments. Such palaces have been excavated beside the mortuary temples of Seti I at Kurna, the Ramasseum of Ramses II and the temple of Ramses III at Medinet Habu. The largest and best preserved of these is the latter, which lies to the south; it comprises a complex of state chambers, living quarters and storerooms. While the pharaoh was in residence on the necropolis, he undoubtedly also watched the progress being made on the excavation and decoration of his tomb in the Valley of the Kings, and on his funerary furniture and equipment.

A large community of labourers and craftsmen, who resided near the temple of Deir el Medina, were engaged on this work. The French Institute of Oriental Archeology have completed a unique 50-year study of this village. From some 40,000 pieces of pottery and scraps of papyrus, they have been able to trace the family histories of each of the inhabitants throughout a span of nearly three centuries: their daily activities, religious ceremonies, marriages, pride in their work, and even their antagonisms and jealousies. The village comprised about eighty families, each possessing a small, uniform and sparsely furnished house. They worked under a strict system of administration and the people were classified according to their work. The designers and scribes were considered superior to the artists, painters and draughtsmen. The quarrymen and masons naturally came above the porters, diggers and mortar mixers. At the bottom of the scale were the watchmen and refreshment carriers. At the top, in charge of the whole community, were the Director of Works and the various foremen immediately under his control.

Attendance was strictly marked and an absent worker had to account for himself. The written excuses have survived the centuries. One had to 'visit my mother-in-law'. Another had to get urgent supplies from the market. Illness was a frequent excuse. The scandals, quarrels and complaints of the workers were all recorded. On one occasion a complaint reached the authorities that a chair, a box and a mirror were missing from the tomb of a worker. He described them in detail. A check was made. Nothing was found. But when Bruyère, leading the French Egyptological Expedition, was excavating the area he found the three described pieces in one of the small tombs in the surrounding cliffs where the dead of the village were buried!

There were also complaints of a more serious nature, as for example the backlog of salaries which led to the famous *Revolution of the 20th/21st Dynasties*, written on papyri and recording that the authorities failed to give allowances to the people of the village for two months. Payment normally came regularly each month in the form of charcoal, dried meat, fish, bandages and cloth, along with materials for their work. When the caravan failed to turn up the villagers staged a revolt and attempted to send representatives in protest to Thebes. They were stopped from crossing the river. However, they did finally send the Omdah (headman) of the village to speak on their behalf and were consequently promised their salaries within a week.

The men of the village were all skilled workers. Those that toiled in the Valley of the Kings for ten day stretches slept in make-shift shelters in a mountain pass above the village until their term of work was over. On their return they had ample time to enjoy sculpting at leisure, making jewellery, household objects and statues of their own guardian deity, Hathor, to whom they built a small shrine. One village resident, Kha, a draughtsman who rose to the position of architect, placed in his tomb a selection of furniture which appears unused. It is doubtful whether he actually enjoyed these luxuries in his home. They were evidently placed in his tomb that they might ensure him a better after-life.

It is strange to note that nowhere on the Theban necropolis have the ruins of a mummification centre yet been found.

Note: *Tickets to tombs and mortuary temples on the necropolis must be purchased from the Ticket Kiosk at the Landing Stage on the western bank of the Nile.*

# CHAPTER 5  THE NECROPOLIS MORTUARY TEMPLES

## BACKGROUND

As we have seen, the reigning Pharaoh was the embodiment of the Sun-god and the God of the Imperial Age. When he died and Amon cast his protective shield over his successor, the cult of the deceased Pharaoh was continued in his mortuary temple, which was also dedicated to Amon.

The largest of these temples, that of Amenhotep III, is no more; all that remain are the twin statues known as the Colossi of Memnon seated in solitary isolation in the plain. The mortuary temple of Seti I at Kurna contains some of the most exquisite relief work on the Theban necropolis. The most beautiful, Queen Hatshepsut's at Deir el Bahri, lies slightly inland from the semi-circle along the valley's edge. The Ramasseum of Ramses II is a page in history, and Medinet Habu, the name given to a group of buildings begun in the 18th Dynasty and continuing to Roman times, includes a splendid temple built by Ramses III on the same pattern as the Ramasseum.

## MORTUARY TEMPLE OF SETI I (KURNA): Plan 11

Seti I was the Pharaoh who fought against the Libyans, Syrians and Hittites in an effort to win back the empire of Thutmose III. He succeeded in reconquering territories spreading from Mesopotamia to the island of Cyprus and carried home vast treasures to adorn his temples, both this one at Kurna and the marvellous one at Abydos. Seti encouraged art and architecture, and his two temples without doubt hold some of the most exquisite relief work in the entire Nile Valley.

Whilst approaching this 19th Dynasty mortuary temple it would be as well to remember that the execution of funerary art was inherited from long-established traditions and was considered sacred. Similar themes and unvarying treatment followed from one dynasty to the next, the only real difference lying in the competence of its execution. It is here that the real value of this temple lies. The

73

**Plan 11**
**MORTUARY TEMPLE OF SETI I (KURNA)**

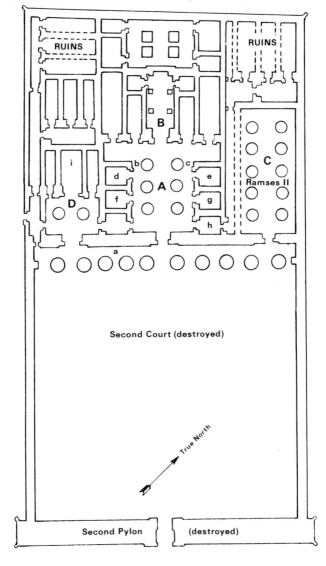

RUINS

RUINS

B

C

Ramses II

i

b c

d e

A

f g

D

h

a

Second Court (destroyed)

True North

Second Pylon (destroyed)

reliefs show that craftsmanship had reached a remarkable stage of maturity. There is little doubt that the artists in Seti's reign were aware of foreshortening and knew how to cope with it. Yet they interpreted their figures as did the artists of the Old Kingdom, never violating the pattern of established art. They merely concentrated their efforts on precise and refined detail.

This temple, apart from being constructed to continue the cult of the deceased Pharaoh and to honour Amon, was also built in reverent memory of Seti's father, Ramses I, who died before constructing a temple of his own. It was not completed by Seti I but by his son, Ramses II, who supplied the missing reliefs and inscriptions.

Of the original length of some 158 metres only about 47 metres of the temple remain, mostly the area containing the sanctuary, its halls and ante-chambers. Most of the frontal courts and pylons are in ruin but, because of the execution of the reliefs, a visit is immensely worthwhile. For example, just beyond the eight remaining columns of the colonnade are three doors leading to the inner part of the temple. The walls between, at (a), carry representations of the provinces of Upper Egypt—a man and a woman alternately—bearing dishes laden with flowers, cakes and wine (to the left) and similar representations of Lower Egypt (to the right). On their heads the former have lotuses, the emblem of Upper Egypt. The latter have papyri, that of Lower Egypt. Above the left-hand relief the Pharaoh offers incense to the barge of Amon carried by priests. And above the right-hand relief he appears before various deities. It is immediately apparent that the lines are sensitive and refined while the drawing is boldly executed.

The *hypostyle hall* (*A*) which we enter through the middle doorway has slabs on the roof of the central aisle on which there are flying vultures, the winged sun-disc and the names of Seti I between two vertical rows of hieroglyphs. Low on the walls Seti I and Ramses II are seen before various deities. At (*b*) and (*c*) are Mut and Hathor, nourishing Seti.

On each side of the hypostyle hall are three chambers. The last two on each side, (*d*) (*e*) (*f*) and (*g*), have fine reliefs which depict Seti offering incense or performing ceremonies in the presence of the deities. In chamber (*d*) Thoth, the god of science, can be seen before the sacred barge of the Pharaoh (on the left-hand wall) while (on the right-hand wall) the Pharaoh is seated before an offering table. On the rear wall Seti is depicted as the god Osiris, seated in a shrine surrounded by deities. Chamber (*h*) bears the sunken, cruder reliefs of Ramses II, who enters the temple (to the right) and offers symbols to Amon, Mut and Khonsu (to the left).

Beyond the hypostyle hall is the *sanctuary* (*B*) which has four simple square pillars, and the decorations on the side walls depict Seti I offering incense before the barge of Amon. The base of Amon's sacred barge still stands here. The chambers beyond are in ruin.

In the right-hand division of the temple is a long hall of Ramses II (*C*). Again we can compare these sunken reliefs with those of the main building. They are clearly far inferior work.

On the corresponding left-hand division of the temple is a small shrine constructed by Ramses I (*D*) and probably usurped by Ramses II. Adjoining it are three chambers. In the middle one (*i*) Seti offers incense to the barge of Amon and, on the rear wall, is a stele shaped like a door, to Ramses II, who appears in Osiris form presided over by Isis as a hawk. The two flanking chambers have reliefs dating from Ramses II and show him before the deities.

## MORTUARY TEMPLE OF QUEEN HATSHEPSUT (DEIR EL BAHRI): Plan 12

### Introduction

Framed by steep cliffs and poised in elegant relief, stands the temple of Deir el Bahri. Justly deserving of its name 'Most Splendid of All', it was the inspiration of the beautiful Queen Makere Hatshepsut, daughter of Thutmose I. What strikes one first when approaching this temple is its unity with nature. Far from being belittled by the stark purity of the cliffs behind, the temple was so designed that the cliffs form a backcloth.

Hatshepsut, whose royal lineage to the Great Royal Wife Ahmose made her the only lawful heir among Thutmose I's children, his sons being by minor wives, was prevented by her sex from succeeding as Pharaoh. She consequently married her half-brother Thutmose II. During his reign and her subsequent co-regency with Thutmose III she retained power in her capable hands.

To appreciate the temple of Deir el Bahri one must know a little of the character of the beautiful woman who conceived it. She was indisputably iron-willed and not willing to let the fact that she was a woman stand in her way. She assumed a throne name — Makere. She wore a royal skirt and ceremonial beard, the badges of kingship. She proved her right to the throne in numerous reliefs of her divine birth.

Once Hatshepsut had secured her right to the throne she embarked on the building of temples and monuments and also on the restoration of damaged sanctuaries. This was perhaps especially important to her since she could hardly record her name in history through military conquest and sought to do so through architectural magnificence. The obelisks she had erected in Karnak temple (page 51) were so placed that the glittering tips should 'inundate the Two Lands just as it appears in the horizon of heaven'. And she planned her mortuary temple to be no less spectacular. Her architect Senmut, whilst drawing inspiration from the adjacent 11th Dynasty temple of the Pharaohs Mentuhotep II and III, carried it out on a very much larger scale. Adopting the idea of the terrace and adding an extra tier, he made such imposing use of it that he deserves special credit. He designed a terraced sanctuary comprising courts, one above the other with connecting inclined planes at the centre. Shrines were dedicated to Hathor and Anubis and chambers devoted to the cult of the queen and her parents.

It was a labour of love, for Senmut, who first entered the service of Hatshepsut as tutor to her daughter Nefrure, had ambitions and abilities that took him high on the ladder of success. He not only ended with no fewer than forty titles but conducted himself as a member of the royal family, enjoying privileges and prerogatives never before enjoyed by a man of humble birth. He was Hatshepsut's supporter and lover and doubtless also her political adviser. He was also granted a privilege accorded to no official before or after: that of constructing his tomb near the mortuary temple of his monarch.

Hatshepsut had two tombs. Her body was found in neither. The first she had dug in the Valley of the Kings where all members of the royal family were laid to rest in the 18th Dynasty. The second, after she became monarch, was in the Taket Zeid Valley, south of Deir el Bahri and overlooking the Valley of the Kings. The former tomb was so designed that the corridors, burrowed 213 metres beneath the barrier hill, should lead to the tomb chamber itself directly beneath the mortuary temple. It was as though, while wishing to construct her tomb in the royal valley, she wanted at the same time to conform to the ancient practice of linking the tomb with the mortuary temple. She never achieved her goal. Bad rock or other causes led to the passage being continued in a swerve 98 metres below ground level and then abandoned. It is devoid of relief and inscription and, apart from limestone slabs relating chapters from the Book of the Dead in red and black sketch form, is a rather pathetic and crude passage. In her red sandstone sarcophagus the body of her father Thutmose I had been laid to rest, until the priests of the 20th Dynasty removed his mummy to the shaft of Deir el Bahri (page 84) for safekeeping. In fact Hatshepsut's sarcophagus had been enlarged to receive his body. Why was Thutmose I laid to rest in his daughter's tomb? Because his own had already been used by Thutmose II, who died prematurely after a short co-regency with Hatshepsut. And Hatshepsut's mummy? It probably suffered the same fate as her statues and representations in murals. For, when Thutmose III finally asserted himself and expelled her from the throne, his years of frustrated energy swelled forth in a campaign of destruction when he obliterated from every temple throughout the land, but from Deir el Bahri in particular, every reference to the female Pharaoh.

Later, when Akhenaten removed references to Amon from the temples of Egypt, the inscriptions of Deir el Bahri were further mutilated. Ramses II endeavoured to restore them but the workmanship was inferior. And in this condition the beautiful temple remained, with only minor alterations taking place until Christian

The Mortuary Temple of Queen Hatshepsut at Deir el Bahri.

# 78

## MORTUARY TEMPLE OF HATSHEPSUT   Plan 12
(Deir el Bahri)

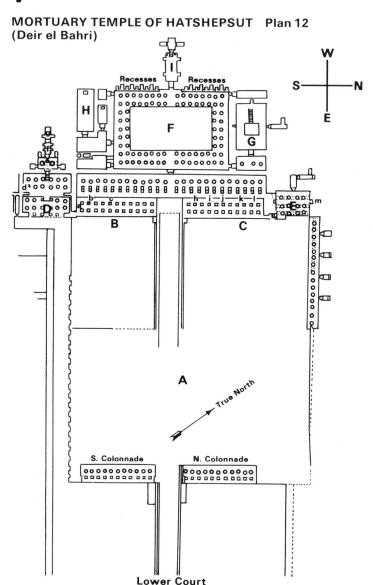

monks set up a convent there. Sadly, but understandably, they too scraped the walls and added to the overall desecration.

Two of the learned members of Napoleon's expedition to Egypt in 1798 first made the temple of Deir el Bahri known to the modern world, releasing part of it from its sandy embrace. Champollion was responsible for deciphering the hieroglyphics and attempting to unravel the family feud. Mariette interpreted the picturesque reliefs of the Voyage to Punt. In 1894 the Egyptian Exploration Fund started to exhume the temple properly but their work was not completed for nine years. Some of the colonnades were roofed in and certain other necessary alterations were carried out to preserve the remaining reliefs and colonnades.

For several years now a Polish team has been excavating and reconstructing the temple. In 1969 they unearthed a small temple built by Thutmose III to the left of the upper terrace of Hatshepsut's temple and parallel with the rock-hewn inner chambers. In 1970 they unearthed what at first appeared to be another terrace but has since been described as a protective roof to the rear of the temple to safeguard against falling rock. (See Work in Progress, No. 13).

### Lower and Central Courts

We ascend the temple of Deir el Bahri from the *lower court* where two colonnades have been restored. These comprise twenty-two columns on each side arranged in double rows. In the southern colonnade is a scene showing two obelisks being transported by water (those Hatshepsut had erected at Karnak). The first row shows them on the deck of the barge and below a trumpeter leads a group of archers to the inauguration ceremony.

Passing between the two colonnades we come to the *central court* (Plan 12 *A*), which leads to the upper terrace. We are now faced with two famous colonnades. On the left (*B*) is the Colonnade of the Expedition to Punt. On the right (*C*) is the Birth Colonnade.

### Punt Colonnade

The Punt Colonnade commemorates an expedition ordered by Queen Hatshepsut to the Land of Punt (in the East Africa/Somalia area) to bring back myrrh and incense trees to be planted on the terraces of the temple. The relief tells us that Amon himself ordered the expedition and it appears that Hatshepsut not only carried out the divine will but made the expedition a major mission.

On the southern wall (*a*) we can see the village in Punt where the houses are constructed over water with ladders leading up to the entrances. We can see the mayor of the city, the inhabitants, the grazing cattle and even the village dog. The Egyptian envoy and his entourage are greeted in welcome and are shown presenting merchandise for barter. The fat, deformed queen of Punt is there. The hieroglyphics relate that this illustrious monarch travelled by donkey and, with obvious wit, the artists have shown the little donkey itself. Throughout the span of Egyptian history, from pre-dynastic times to the fall of the empire, it was not often that deformed or physically handicapped persons were sculpted or drawn. The few that were belonged to the earlier dynasties and were people of the lower classes. The portrayal of the queen of Punt suffering from the swollen legs of elephantiasis, and without even a royal carriage for transport, makes one feel that neither Hatshepsut nor her artists had much respect for her.

On the back wall at (b) the Egyptian fleet sets sail, arrives in Punt and we see the transportation of the incense trees planted in small tubs (top row) and on board the vessel (lower row). These will be carried back to Deir el Bahri, there to be planted in the court. In fact the roots are still on site to this day.

One cannot but feel, divine will notwithstanding, that more than a little of Hatshepsut's whim and fancy went into the elaboration of the whole mission. In a joyous representation at the centre of the long back wall (c) the queen (defaced) can be seen offering the fruits of her expedition to Amon: incense trees, wild game, cattle, electrum and bows. The whole mural speaks of success and pleasure.

**Shrine of Hathor**
To the left of the Colonnade of Punt stands the Shrine of Hathor (D). It has two roofed-in colonnades with Hathor columns leading to the shrine itself which comprises three chambers, one behind the other, and each with several recesses. In the colonnaded court is a large sacrificial scene on the southern wall (d) showing a boat containing the Hathor-cow with Queen Hatshepsut drinking from the udder. On the rear western wall is a representation of Thutmose II (replacing Hatshepsut) having his hand licked by the Hathor-cow.

In the first chamber (e) Hatshepsut or Thutmose III is represented with several of the deities. The colour is excellent, especially on the ceiling which is decorated with stars on a blue sky. The second room (f) shows Hatshepsut (scraped) making offerings to Hathor, who stands on the sacred barge beneath the canopy. This is a relief of unusual beauty. Ehi, son of Horus, is the little nude boy who

Hathor column from the shrine of Hathor, Deir el Bahri.

holds a sistrum in front of the queen. The third room (*g*) has an unusual pointed roof and the wall reliefs show Hatshepsut (on each of the side walls) drinking from the udder of the cow, Hathor, with Amon standing before them. On the back wall is another particularly beautiful relief of Hatshepsut standing between Hathor and Amon with the latter holding before her face the hieroglyph symbol of life.

### Birth Colonnade

The Birth Colonnade corresponds exactly to the Punt Colonnade. As already mentioned, it was constructed to allay concern about Hatshepsut's right to the throne. The theory of divine origin was above discussion, let alone dispute, and this is shown in a scene of the ram-headed Khnum shaping Hatshepsut and her *ka* on the potter's wheel (*h*) under instructions from Amon who has impregnated the queen mother. Among the particularly fine representations is that of the queen mother Ahmose (*i*), full with child. She radiates joy and stands dignified in her pregnancy, smiling a smile of supreme contentment as she is led to the birth room. Unfortunately most of the scene in which Amon and the queen mother are borne to the heavens by two goddesses seated on a lion-headed couch, is badly damaged. But the grotesque figure of the god Bes can be seen in the lower row (*j*).

In the scene of the actual birth the queen mother sits on a chair which is placed on a couch held aloft by various gods. This in turn stands upon another couch also supported by gods. The queen mother has a retinue of female attendants. Hathor then presents Hatshepsut to Amon and the twelve *kas* of the divine child are suckled by twelve goddesses (*k*). Hatshepsut and her *ka* have been erased but in the scene at the end of the wall (*l*) they pass through the hands of various goddesses who record the divine birth. Hatshepsut's mother is shown in the presence of the ibis-headed Thoth, the ram-headed Khnum and the frog-headed Heket. She also converses with Amon who tells her that her daughter shall exercise kingship throughout the land.

By depicting Hatshepsut as a boy and by repeating the theme of Amon laying a hand of blessing on her shoulder, the most important prejudices against her rule are overcome.

### Small and Upper Courts, Sanctuary

To the right of the Birth Colonnade is a small court (*E*) comprising twelve sixteen-sided columns in three rows, and leading to the chapel of Anubis, which has three chambers. The walls of the court have excellently preserved reliefs, though representations of the queen have all been damaged. On the right-hand wall (*m*) above the small recess is a scene of the monarch making a wine-offering to the hawk-headed Sokaris, god of the dead. On the rear wall offerings are made to Amon (to the left) and Anubis (to the right) with the sacrificial gifts heaped up before each.

The *Upper Court* (*F*) was the part of the temple that suffered most severely at the hands of the Christian monks. It has been closed to visitors for some years for reconstruction. It includes a small vestibule leading to one of the few altars (*G*) to come down to us from antiquity on their original sites, and to a sacrificial hall (*H*) with reliefs adorning the walls. At the back of the court are a number of small recesses, some larger than others, and the central recess leads into the sanctuary itself which was cut directly into the cliff backing the temple. The granite portal forming the entrance dates from the time of the Ptolemies.

The *Sanctuary* (*I*) comprises three chambers. The first two have vaulted ceilings and adjoining recesses. In the first chamber is a scene (on the upper reaches of the right-hand wall) of Hatshepsut, Thutmose III and their little daughter, Princess Ranofru, sacrificing to the barge of Amon. Behind them are the queen's father Thutmose I with his wife Ahmose and their little daughter Bitnofru. A similar scene, somewhat damaged, is represented on the left-hand wall, with Thutmose III kneeling. In the inner room of the sanctuary the reliefs show a marked deterioration from the worthy representations in the reign of Hatshepsut. This room was restored by Euergetes II.

As already mentioned, Hatshepsut's mummy was never found. It was neither in the tomb she constructed in the Valley of the Kings, nor in the one excavated south of the mortuary temple, though it has been suggested that her body may be one of the couple of 'unknown women' from the shaft at Deir el Bahri. Whether she was poisoned that Thutmose III might take over the throne, stabbed by her lover, killed by officials jealous of Senmut's favour, or died a natural death remains a matter for speculation.

DEIR EL BAHRI—SHAFT AND CAVERN

## The Shaft at Deir el Bahri

In 1881 a twelve metre shaft was excavated at the foot of the precipitous cliffs to the north of Deir el Bahri. It was found to contain no less than forty mummies of Egypt's ancient monarchs, all of which now lie in the Egyptian Museum in Cairo.

The story of this discovery goes back to 1876, when various antique objects began to appear on the market at Luxor, slowly at first but with a steadily increasing flow. Obviously some royal tomb was being ransacked. Enquiries—some subtle, some otherwise— yielded nothing. Although the *felaheen* of Kurna were clearly involved it was also abundantly clear that they intended to keep quiet. When funerary statuettes of King Pinedjem followed the flow of important papyri on the market the Director of Antiquities, Sir Gaston Maspero, redoubled his efforts in search of a solution.

The only substantial clue seemed to lead to a prominent antiquities merchant, Abd el Rasool Ahmed. Yet even when his sullen silence was broken and he agreed to a cross-examination, it led nowhere. His talent for denial was masterly. And, since he was such a respected citizen with so many supporters who could vouch for his honesty and innocence, there was complete deadlock.

Ironically enough it was a family rivalry that led to his betrayal. His eldest brother finally led Emile Brugsch, in the absence of Maspero, to the site. A shaft was found in one of the coves of the range of hills separating the Valley of the Kings from Deir el Bahri. In the words of Maspero himself it was: 'A catacomb crammed with Pharaohs!' It included some of the most famous kings of the 18th and 19th Dynasties such as Amenhotep I, Thutmose II, Thutmose III, Seti I, Ramses II and Ramses III. One of the mummies was that of Sekenenre, an Egyptian prince during the time of the Hyksos. Mummification had been carried out only after some decomposition had set in and it showed that he had met an extremely violent death; his jaw was crushed and there were signs of three other blows, each of which could have been fatal, on the head. Merneptah, thought by some scholars to be the Pharaoh of the Exodus, was missing. Drowned in the Red Sea? Many thought so until 1898 when his mummy turned up with twelve others in the tomb of Amenhotep II, where they had also been hidden by the priests for safety.

These hiding-places represent a pathetic last attempt to safeguard the bodies of Egypt's deceased Pharaohs from robbery. That the hidden Valley of the Kings was no safer than the huge pyramids was quickly made evident. And when the country experienced Akhenaten's reformation, tomb-robbing became a free-for-all, especially in the desolate Valley of the Kings, and with every indication of official connivance. At the beginning of the 19th Dynasty Haremhab issued instructions for the reburial of Thutmose IV. His successors Seti I and Ramses II endeavoured to enforce better security but the situation became worse as central authority lapsed under the later Ramessides and violation of the burial places was resumed. The temptation in the form of pure bullion alone was more than enough to turn desire into an epidemic of greed. One has only to see the solid gold coffin, gold statuettes, shrines and jewellery of Tutankhamon, whose funerary equipment is now so well known to the world, to have some idea of the lost treasures of the necropolis.

When robbers were caught in ancient times they were duly tried and punished. Two papyri, known as the Abbott and Amherst papyri after their discoverers, not only confirm this but give details of the transportation of the mummies to the obscure shaft at Deir el Bahri. No less than sixty priests and officials of the necropolis were arrested at the time for complicity in the desecration of the tombs. Abd el Rasool was merely the tail end of a long history of pillage.

### The Cavern at Deir el Bahri

Before leaving Deir el Bahri, mention must be made of a cavern situated on an elevated mountain ledge above the mortuary temple. Though it is not easily accessible, reference is made to it because it was used by the workers on the temple as a resting-place and the walls are covered with sketches and spare-time doodles. They depicted their despised overseer in several unflattering and somewhat crude activities and are valuable as being amongst the few examples of free individual expression. In these sketches the artist not the artisan was at work and the theme was entirely his own.

## MORTUARY TEMPLE OF RAMSES II (THE RAMASSEUM): Plan 13

### Introduction

This magnificent mortuary temple is unfortunately half in ruin. It compares in both construction and quality of material with the mortuary temple of Seti I at Kurna but not in the artistic execution

# 86

## Plan 13
## MORTUARY TEMPLE OF RAMSES II (RAMASSEUM)

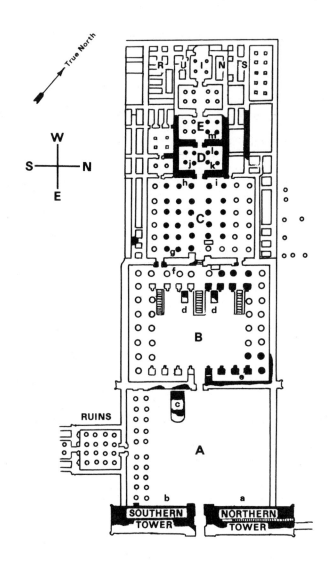

of the murals. The design is simple for a New Kingdom structure
and though Ramses' son Merneptah, and his successor Ramses III,
made some additions, they were minimal and did not detract from
Ramses II's original architectural conception.

Ramses II developed what can only be described as an extraordinary building activity during his 67-year reign. He enjoyed having
his state sculptors depict him repeatedly and there is hardly a pylon,
hall or chamber in the temples of Egypt that does not bear his name.
His monuments, mostly massive, spread from Memphis and
Heliopolis to Abydos and Thebes, apart from those in the heart of
Nubia. His image is also perpetuated in gigantic detail in the rocks
of Asia.

One can imagine with what joy his sculptors presented osten-
tatious projects that they were sure would be accepted. The image
of Ramses II is more indelibly projected into the modern age than
any other. His favourite theme was his famous alliance with the
King of the Hittites. It is in fact depicted on the great pylon that
forms the eastern entrance to the Ramasseum. This campaign was
the Pharaoh's only really important one in Asia over some fifteen
years, though he was also responsible for suppressing some Nubian
revolts and carrying out a campaign in Libya.

The entire structure of the Ramasseum within the girdle-wall
measures approximately 275 metres by 168 metres, though a large
portion consisted of subsidiary buildings and storerooms.

### Entrance Pylon

The murals on the inner surfaces of the entrance pylon show, on the
northern tower (*a*) towards the centre of the wall (lower rows), the
Egyptian army on the march with infantry and charioteers. The
Egyptian camp is shown above them with a rampart of shields. This
is a lively scene with the chariots drawn up in long lines and heavy
baggage-waggons with their teams nearby. Some of the unharnessed
horses are being foddered. Some of the soldiers converse with one
another. One drinks from a wineskin. Two others quarrel. The
scene to the right of this same tower shows Ramses II seated on his
throne taking counsel with his princes who stand before him. Below
him is a row of captured spies being beaten to extract information.

On the southern tower (*b*) the actual attack is shown. The entire
left-hand side of the pylon shows the battle of Kadesh (as depicted
also on the pylon of Luxor temple, page 26): Ramses II dashes into
battle in his chariot, dead and wounded cover the ground, others
retreat in confusion only to fall headlong into the Orontes, the

Hittites take refuge in their fortress. The reliefs on the right-hand half of the tower show the Pharaoh grasping enemies by the hair whilst smiting them.

## First and Second Courts

The *first court* of the Ramasseum (*A*) is mostly in ruin. Towards the rear, before the ancient western gate, lie the remains of what was once a *colossus* of the king and one of the most enormous pieces of stone ever shaped to such perfection (*c*). This massive statue, or rather the remains of the chest, upper arm, foot, etc., shows work of superb craftsmanship even to the final polish. When the French expedition under Napoleon visited Egypt careful measurements were made of the various remaining parts and it was estimated that the statue's total height must have been over seventeen metres and its weight over one thousand tons. In other words this granite statue not only exceeded in size the Colossi of Memnon (page 100), but also most of the statues of Ramses' ancestors. Its transportation from the granite quarries of Aswan in one piece is almost impossible to conceive. Hatshepsut's obelisks at Karnak were only one third of the weight.

On passing the colossal remains we enter the *second court* (*B*), which is in a much better state of preservation. It has colonnades on all four sides, those to the rear on a terrace. Facing the court are statues of Osiris and the representations on the column shafts show Ramses II sacrificing to the deities. This court was the one identified with the Augustan historian Diodorus' description of the 'Tomb of Osymandyas'. 'Osymandyas' may be explained as a corrupt form of User-ma-re, one of the names of Ramses II. The two colossal monoliths of the king (*d*), which must once have towered over the pylons of the Ramasseum, inspired Shelley to write his famous sonnet *Ozymandias*.

In this court are well preserved scenes of the battle of Kadesh (*e*). Ramses II dashes into battle (lower row). He is depicted larger than his men, and the enemy, mostly dead and wounded, lie in heaps on the ground. The fortress of Kadesh, surrounded by a moat, divides a group of the enemy from the battlefield. These men, far from preparing themselves for battle, are helping their drowning companions. Though this mural has been considered by some as a pretentious interpretation, there is no doubt that the complexity of the composition shows development and sophistication. The individual figures, however, indicate marked deterioration from the expressive detail of the murals of Seti I's mortuary temple.

Higher on the wall (*e*) are scenes from the Festival of the God Min which was celebrated when the Pharaoh came to the throne. The priests, who stand to the side of the king and await a procession headed by other priests carrying images of the royal ancestors, let forth four birds to carry the royal tidings to the four corners of the earth. Further to the right the Pharaoh cuts a sheaf with a sickle for presenting to the god. Murals portraying such festivals are immensely effective. The artists' ability to depict battle action is less so in view of the stylized treatment of the human form.

At the back of the court are some stairs, and on the rear wall to the left (*f*) are three rows of relief work. The bottom row depicts Ramses II as a family man with his eleven sons. The middle row (left) shows the hawk-headed Montu holding the hieroglyph for life before the king's face and (right) the king kneels before the Theban triad while Thoth, who is behind him, writes his years on a palm-leaf. In the top row he is making a sacrifice to Ptah and offering incense to Min.

Remains of the colossal monolith of Ramses II in his Mortuary Temple, the Ramasseum.

## Hypostyle Hall

The Hypostyle Hall (C), which follows a small flight of stairs at the centre back of the court, is markedly similar to the one at Karnak. Both have three aisles, the taller columns at the centre with calyx capitals and the lower ones at the sides with bud capitals. As at Karnak, the difference in height is made up by a wall with openings for light. The hypostyle hall of the Ramasseum is less cumbersome than that of Karnak. The columns appear more graceful and better proportioned. Throughout the hall the representations depict Ramses II in battle. This time the troops with ladders storm the fortress of Zapur (g—lower row). The Pharaoh dashes into the thick of battle in his chariot (to the left), leaving the enemy in flight or scattered on the ground. To the right the attacking Egyptians scale the fortress on ladders and push up to the walls under the protection of storming-sheds and shields. The sons of the Pharaoh took part and proved themselves worthy of their heroic father. Each is identifiable by his name engraved beside him.

On the western walls (h) and (i) the sons of Ramses II are shown (in the lower rows). Above them (at h) the Pharaoh is followed by a goddess in the presence of Amon and Mut. Above the princes (at i) he is depicted before Amon and Khonsu with the lion-headed Sekhmet behind him.

Beyond the hypostyle hall are two smaller hypostyle halls falling one behind the other in the middle of the remaining chambers which spread backwards and sidewards from the few standing walls. The first (D) has astrological representations on the roof and on the eastern walls (j) and (k) priests bear the sacred boats of Amon, Mut and Khonsu, each decorated with the head of its god. On the rear right-hand wall (l) Ramses is seated beneath the sacred tree of Heliopolis, on the leaves of which his names are being written by Atum, who is seated on a throne to the left, with a goddess and Thoth to the right.

The second hypostyle hall (E) is mostly in ruin. It has some sacrificial representations including a scene (m) of Ramses burning incense to Ptah and the lion-headed Sekhmet.

## The Portrayal of Ramses II

Ramses II will always remain a central figure in Egyptian history and one that can be forgiven for claiming full credit, here and there, for work begun by his ancestors. He was the Pharaoh who dug out the heart of a mountain at Abu Simbel in order to fashion within it a great temple in thanksgiving for his victory over the Hittites.

According to his royal scribe, Pentaur, when he and his chariot driver were separated from the army and hopelessly surrounded by the enemy, the fearless Ramses II six times charged the foe single-handed. He hewed them down with his sword and trampled them under the wheels of his chariot. According to Pentaur, Ramses overthrew 2,500 enemy chariots, scattered 100,000 warriors and drove the rest into the water!

Evidence of Ramses II as a military tactician is often overlooked. He never put local militia in charge of frontier posts. He placed Nubians in the north, sent Delta tribes to the south, placed tribes from the western Delta to the east, and tribes of the eastern Delta were sent to control the west. (These activities were recorded in the Temple at Abu Simbel.)

Ramses II also seems to have been aware of the threat to Egypt from the 'People of the Sea', and, in fact, successfully defended Egypt from them; when excavating a line of fortresses built by Ramses II in the western Delta, Labib Habachi observed this; the great battle against the Sea People only took place in the reign of Ramses II's successor, Ramses III.

Statues of Osiris in the second court of the Ramasseum.

# 92

## MORTUARY TEMPLE OF RAMSES III (MEDINET HABU)

### Introduction

Medinet Habu is the name given by the early Christians to a group of buildings dating from the beginning of the 18th Dynasty and continuing right through to Roman times. The original structure was built by Hatshepsut and Thutmose III as a small, graceful temple (Plan 14 *A*). Ramses III built an unusual entrance structure (*B*) which took the place of the regular entrance pylon and portals of stone. This structure is known as the *Pavilion*, the name given by the French scholars accompanying Napoleon. Ramses III also built a splendid mortuary temple (*C*) which is one of the best examples of the smaller type of sanctuaries of the time. Under the Ptolemies and the Romans the temple was enlarged and the complex elaborated.

We enter the Medinet Habu complex through the Pavilion (*B*), a structure of unusual design, perhaps influenced by the citadels of Syria where Ramses III fought many battles. In front of it are two small watch-towers leading to a battlement of elevated masonry with central doorway. On each side of the doorway are scenes of Ramses slaying his enemies: Nubians and Libyans in the presence of Amon-Ra to the left. Hittites, Sardinians, Sicilians, Philistines and other enemies to the right.

Passing through the entrance we find the high walls on both sides decorated with reliefs, all of a warlike nature, including two representations of the war-goddess Sekhmet, and prisoners of war being recorded by Thoth and the goddess Sefkhet. The scenes in the small rooms of the upper stories (approached from a stairway on the left-hand tower) are of a totally different nature. They show family life, home comforts, and, in one tiny chamber, is the so-called *harem scene*; the women hold flowers and fans, and the seated Ramses III catches hold of the arm of his daughter, while stroking her chin with the other hand.

Passing westwards out of the Pavilion, we pass the shrine of Amenertais (*D*) to the left, and approach the Mortuary Temple.

### The Mortuary Temple of Ramses III

The mortuary temple of Ramses III at Medinet Habu was built on exactly the same plan as the Ramasseum. The paint on the reliefs

**MEDINET HABU COMPLEX    Plan 14**

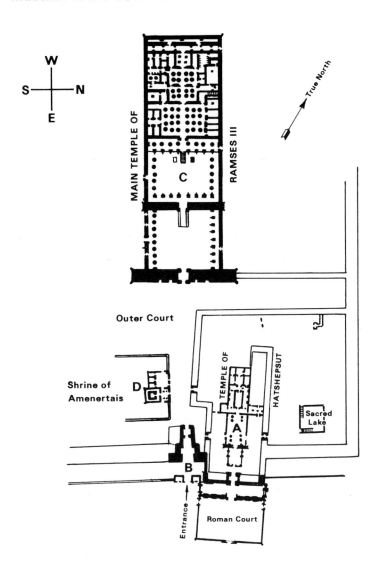

is well preserved, in some places in nearly perfect condition. This temple grew through successive years and, as the campaigns of Ramses were graphically recorded with its growth, his military exploits can be followed step by step from the rear, or in other words from his last military campaign on the foremost pylon, backwards in time.

### First Pylon, First Court

The *first pylon* (Plan 15 *P.1*) is covered on both sides with representations and inscriptions recording Ramses III's victory over the Libyans in the 11th year of his reign. On the right-hand tower (*a*) the Pharaoh stands before Amon (to the right) in the traditional pose of dangling enemies by the hair whilst smiting them with a club. The captured lands — circular forts inscribed with the name of the city and mounted on bound enemies — are handed to him by the hawk-headed Montu. Between the grooves for the flagstaffs (to the left) is a similar scene on a smaller scale, and below it is a long poetic description in exaggerated language of the great victory. At the foot of the pylon Amon is seated (to the left) with Ptah standing behind him inscribing the Pharaoh's name on a palm-leaf. The Pharaoh kneels before Amon and receives from him the hieroglyphs for 'jubilee of the reign' suspended on a palm-branch. Thoth writes the king's years on the leaves of the tree.

The left-hand tower of the entrance pylon repeats these scenes and inscriptions.

Passing through the central portal, which is embellished with representations of Ramses III worshipping the various deities, we enter the *first court* (*A*) and view an interesting representation on the inner side of the first pylon (*b*). This is also of the Libyan campaign. The mercenaries who took part are recognisable by their round helmets ornamented with horns. The charioted Pharaoh charges and overthrows the enemy. This court is flanked by covered colonnades, those to the right with colossal statues of the king as Osiris in front of each. The scenes on the side walls repeat the victorious war themes and the triumphant return of the king with his captives to attend the Great Feast of Amon.

### Second Pylon, Second Court

At the back of the court is the *second pylon* (*P.2*) recording the Pharaoh's battles in the eighth year of his reign. On the left-hand tower (*c*) he leads three rows of prisoners to Amon and Mut. These prisoners do not have beards, which usually denote Asian peoples,

**95**

## Plan 15
## MORTUARY
## TEMPLE
## OF RAMSES III
## (MEDINET HABU)

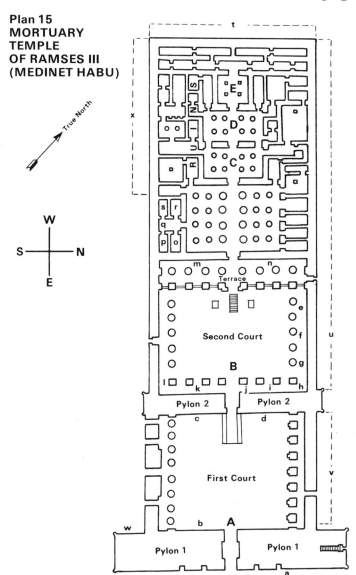

but wear caps adorned with feathers and aprons decorated with tassels. The right-hand tower (*d*) has a long series of inscriptions recording Ramses' military triumph over 'the Great League of Sea-Peoples', probably Sardinians.

An inclined plane leads us through the granite gateway of the second pylon and into the *second court* (*B*), which was the area converted into a church. It was fully cleared of remnants of the Christian period in 1895 and this proved to be one instance where we can thank the early Christians for preserving rather than destroying. For it is due to their having covered the original representations with mud, to avoid distracting the congregation no doubt, that they are in such good condition today. This court is an almost exact replica of the second court of the Ramasseum, both in architectural layout and in the relief drawings. On the back walls of the colonnades are scenes from the life of the Pharaoh including important festivals and warlike deeds.

On the right-hand side of the court (upper rows) are scenes from the Great Festival of the God Min. As in the mural of the Ramasseum, there is a lovely representation including trumpeters, drummers and castanet players. At (*e*) the Pharaoh is borne on a richly-decorated litter with a canopy from the palace, led by priests and soldiers and followed by his sons and courtiers. At the head of the line (upper row) are a trumpeter and a drummer and in the lower row castanet players. At (*f*) the king sacrifices before the image of Min and offers incense. Then comes a scene of the sacred procession: it starts on the right-hand wall at (*g*) and continues round the corner to (*h*). Studying the scene from left to right, we see priests, flanked by fan-bearers; the priests carry the image of Min on a litter. Next more priests with the sacred caskets. Then come the Pharaoh, the sacred white bull of Min, priests, the queen and a procession of priests in two rows carrying standards and images of the Pharaoh and his ancestors. Further to the right the Pharaoh awaits the procession and the priests allow four birds to fly to the four corners of the earth to carry the royal tidings. At (*i*) the Pharaoh cuts a sheaf of corn with his sickle in the presence of priests and his queen (above). The white bull again appears in front of the Pharaoh and beneath is a series of images of royal ancestors. At (*j*) the Pharaoh is shown offering incense to the god Min as he stands beneath a canopy.

The *colonnade* on the left-hand side of the court has scenes from the Festival of Ptah-Sokaris in the upper rows, and the much more interesting war reliefs in the lower divisions on the wall, starting

Second Pylon of the Temple of Ramses III at Medinet Habu.

with the inner wall of the second pylon (*k*). The first scene shows
the Pharaoh attacking the Libyans with his charioteers as he shoots
with his bow and the infantry flee in all directions. The mercenaries
are in the lower row. The second scene shows him returning from
battle with three rows of fettered Libyans before him and two fan-
bearers behind. The third scene shows him leading his prisoners of
war before Amon and Mut. These are themes we have met before,
particularly on the first pylon of Ramses III's little temple in the
court of Karnak (page 41), but with the addition of an interesting
scene in the corner (*l*). This shows the Pharaoh turning in his chariot
to receive four rows of prisoners of war from, amongst other no-
tables, his own sons. Hands and phalluses (uncircumcised) of the
slain are counted.

The rear walls of the terrace (*m*) and (*n*) have three rows of
representations. In the two upper rows the Pharaoh is shown worshipping various deities. The lowest row depicts the royal princes
and princesses.

### Great Hypostyle Hall

The Great Hypostyle Hall follows. The roof was originally supported by twenty-four columns in six rows of four, with the eight
columns forming the double central row considerably thicker than
the others. The wall reliefs show Ramses III in the presence of
various deities. Adjoining each side of the hypostyle hall are a series
of chambers which stored costly jewels, musical instruments, etc.
Ramses III was the last of the great Pharaohs and also the weal-
thiest. As he offers the fruits of earlier conquests, coupled with his
own, to Amon, one can see that this is no exaggeration. In chamber
(*o*) he presents Amon with papyrus-holders in the form of lions with
the Pharaoh's head or kneeling figures of the Pharaoh. In chamber
(*p*) costly vessels, with lids of rams', hawks', or Pharaohs' heads, are
handed to Amon. Chamber (*q*) shows the Pharaoh handing Amon
sacks of precious stones and in (*r*) costly table-services, harps, silver,
lead and ornaments. Again, in chamber (*s*) he offers heaps of gold
and other precious metals to Amon. The chambers to the right of
the hypostyle hall contain mostly sacrificial scenes before the
various deities.

Beyond the hypostyle hall are three smaller chambers (*C*, *D* and
*E*). The first two have eight columns each and the third has four
pillars. The surrounding chambers are dedicated to different
deities.

## Exterior

On the outside of the temple there are important historical reliefs commemorating the wars of Ramses III. Those on the western wall (*t*) have scenes of the Pharaoh's battle against the Nubians. The actual battle scene, the triumphal procession with captives and the presentation to Amon, are shown. The northern wall has ten scenes from the wars against the Libyans and a naval victory over a northern people. The naval battle (at *u*) is an extremely animated representation: having alighted from his chariot the Pharaoh shoots against the hostile fleet. Before him are archers. Above him, in the form of a vulture, hovers the goddess of Lower Egypt. One enemy ship has capsized and the Egyptian vessels—distinguishable by a lion's head on the prow—are steered by men with large oars whilst the rest of the crew row from benches. There are bound captives inside the ship. Others appear in the lower row. The northern wall (at *v*) has scenes from the Syrian wars including the storming of a fortress and the presentation of prisoners to Amon and Khonsu.

There is little doubt that these reliefs show a decline in artistic

Ramses III presents wine to the deities. Scene from his Mortuary Temple at Medinet Habu.

ability. The painstaking detail of Seti I's reliefs is lost. These are cruder in execution and the composition is somewhat lackadaisical compared to the relief work of the 18th Dynasty. There is, however, one relief that reflects artistic inheritance from earlier times. This is the hunt for deer, wild bull and wild asses in a marshy area, and it can be seen on the southern wall on the back of the first pylon (*w*). The Pharaoh has already slain one bull which lies on the ground. Others escape into the thicket and the artist has endeavoured to create depth by showing the bull hiding between the rushes. As a three-dimensional approach it is extremely effective. On the southern wall (at *x*) is a *festival calendar* which includes a list of appointed sacrifices dating from Ramses III's accession to the throne. (See Work in Progress No. 5).

## COLOSSI OF MEMNON

Two massive statues, sadly weathered by time and now of no artistic merit, sit in stately isolation in the fertile lower valley of the necropolis. They once formed an impressive entrance to the mortuary temple of Amenhotep III and are solitary relics of his golden era. The mortuary temple itself was probably destroyed by a high flood. Some of the blocks were re-used by Merneptah, son of Ramses II, in his neighbouring mortuary temple.

These two statues rise to a height of twenty metres above the plain. They were made of quartzite under the supervision of the Pharaoh's chief architect, Amenhotep son of Hapu, who transported them from the quarries on eight barges along the Nile during the annual flood. The one on the left is in a better state of repair and shows Amenhotep III seated and flanked by his mother Metamwa and his wife Tiy. A third figure between the legs has been destroyed. On each side of the seat are representations of two Nile-gods winding the papyrus and lotus, symbols of Lower and Upper Egypt, round the hieroglyph for 'unite'.

The so-called Colossi of Memnon is a misnomer, since the Romans referred to one statue only, the northern one, as the Colossus of Memnon, the legendary son of Aurora, goddess of the dawn. Memnon had slain Antilochus during the Trojan War—the latter being the valiant son of Nestor—and had himself finally fallen at the hand of Achilles. The first visitors to the necropolis during the Roman epoch interpreted the strange sounds they heard emerging from the statues at dawn each day as Memnon greeting his mother Aurora.

The myth grew and tourists flocked to see and hear for themselves. The number of Greek and Latin inscriptions, in both prose and verse, on the legs of the statues, attest to each having heard the sound for himself. Some said it was a musical note, others a trumpet blast. Others still said that they could hear voices chanting, or the sound of an angry god. It was a great tourist attraction. The curious were subsequently followed by the eminent. Physicists came — and exploded the myth utterly. It was, they said, the contracting of the stone during the cool nights following expansion during the day that caused a splitting off of particles from the surface.

Be that as it may the sound completely stopped when, in the time of Septimius Severus, the upper part of the northern statue was repaired and some of the holes were filled in. It has never been heard since. Tourists in Roman times said the sound had stopped because Memnon was unhappy!

The Colossi of Memnon.

## VALLEY OF THE KINGS

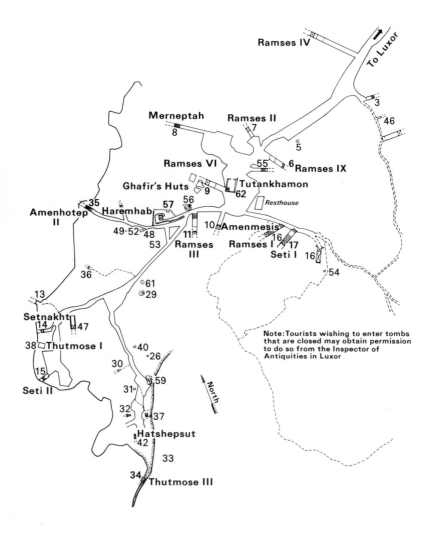

Ramses IV

To Luxor

3

46

Merneptah
8

Ramses II
7

5

Ramses VI

55 6 Ramses IX

Ghafir's Huts

Tutankhamon

9 62

Resthouse

Amenhotep
II

35

Haremhab

57 56

49-52 48

53

11

10 Amenmesis

16

Ramses I

Seti I 17

16

Ramses
III

54

36

61
29

13

Setnakht

14 47

38 Thutmose I

40
26

30

15

59

Seti II

31

32

37

Hatshepsut
42

33

34 Thutmose III

North

Note: Tourists wishing to enter tombs
that are closed may obtain permission
to do so from the Inspector of
Antiquities in Luxor

## CHAPTER 6    THE NECROPOLIS
## THE VALLEY OF THE KINGS

### BACKGROUND

The Valley of the Kings, otherwise known as *Biban el Muluk*, is situated about two miles inland from the edge of the valley. A tarmac road makes the distance seem short. Before its construction a visitor had a sense of the arid remoteness of the site chosen by the Pharaohs of the 18th, 19th and 20th Dynasties for their tombs. There are over sixty in the valley.

The Pharaohs of the New Kingdom, as already explained, chose to separate their tombs from their mortuary temples as a safeguard against pillage, and to burrow through solid rock in an effort to ensure eternal seclusion. The actual tomb design was relatively uniform, differing only in length and in the number of chambers. There were usually three corridors, one following the other, leading to the inner chambers. High up on the walls of the second corridor were sometimes oblong recesses for the reception of the furniture and effects of the deceased. Alternatively other recesses or chambers were provided at the end of the third corridor for the same purpose. At the end of the third corridor was a door leading to an ante-chamber; the main hall or tomb chamber lay beyond. The roof of the tomb chamber was often supported by pillars and small chambers led off it. In the centre or to the rear was a crypt containing the sarcophagus, usually of red sandstone.

A shaft, sometimes dropping to a depth of over six metres, was a feature of several tombs. Whether this was designed to discourage possible grave-robbers from proceeding further is not sure, though there are positive indications that this was their purpose; for example, the representations on the upper walls of the pit shaft were usually left unfinished with the outer frame of decoration missing, whereas the chambers beyond the shaft were fully decorated. Another theory is that the shaft was for the drainage of rain water; though rain is not common in Egypt the tomb designers may well have taken precautions against the possibility of seepage.

The concern of the Pharaoh was not with his death, which was inevitable, but that his journey to the hereafter should be as smooth as possible. There was no apprehension, no fear. Man continued life after death in much the same manner as he had lived on earth, so long as the necessities for his existence were provided, safeguards were taken to prevent his body from decay, and the religious formulae were scrupulously followed.

In the Middle Kingdom the religious formulae by which the dead were to triumph had been recorded both inside and outside the sarcophagus. Gradually the texts were elaborated and scrolls of papyrus were placed in the coffin as well. Enlarged over the years these gradually became uniform and the nucleus of what has become known as the *Book of the Dead*.

The rock-hewn passages and chambers represent stages in the journey to the underworld, which was supposedly divided into twelve hours or caverns. The deceased sailed through them at night in the boat of the Sun-god—in fact actually absorbed by him— and representations on the first corridors of the tombs often show the ram-headed Sun-god surrounded by his retinue who are standing in a boat and temporarily bringing light to the places he traverses. As they pass from one leg of the journey to another they have to go through massive gates, each guarded by huge serpents. These chapters of the formula are know as the *Book of the Gates*.

The forward corridors were generally devoted to *Praises of Ra* —hymns to be sung and illustrations of the ceremonies to be performed before the statue of the deceased Pharaoh to imbue it with eternal life. And finally the deceased reached the judgement seat of Osiris, King of the Underworld.

Osiris, the creator of law and agriculture, had once ruled on earth. With his wife and sister Isis at his side he had been a just and much loved ruler who was slain by his jealous brother Set. Set, as the myth goes, conspired against Osiris and at a banquet persuaded him to enter a chest which was then sealed and thrown into the Nile. It was carried down to the sea. The broken-hearted Isis wandered far and wide in tortured misery seeking the body of her loved one. Accompanied on her sad mission by the goddess Nephthys she eventually found the body entangled in a tamarisk bush in the marshes of the delta. She hid the body, but Set, out boar-hunting, found it and cut it into fourteen pieces, scattering it in all directions. Isis continued her mission, collected the pieces (at each spot a monument was erected, which accounts for the widespread myth) and sought the help of the jackal-god Anubis, who became god of embalmment, to prepare it for the netherworld. While he carried out her orders Isis wept and prayed and drew near her dead lord 'making a shadow with her pinions and causing a wind with her wings . . . raising the weary limbs of the silent-hearted (dead), receiving his seed, and bringing forth an heir . . .'[1]

Isis, the myth continues, raised her son Horus in the marshes until he was strong enough to avenge his father's death by slaying Set. He then set out to seek his father and raise him from the dead. The risen Osiris, however, could no longer reign in the kingdom on earth and now became king of the underworld where, with Isis still at his side, he ruled below with the same justice as he had exercised above. Horus took over the throne of his father on earth.

On the walls of the tomb chamber, or in the rear corridors, are dramatic representations of the dangers carefully guarded against: enemies withdrawing the breath from the nostrils of the deceased; water bursting into flame as he drinks; foes robbing him of his throne, his organs and, worst of all, his very name, which would thus deprive him forever of his identity.

The tombs in the Valley of the Kings, which are guidebooks to the hereafter, give us an insight into the hopes, expectations and fears of the living Pharaoh. Very soon after his coronation he must have ordered the construction of these usually vast complexes. His artists made initial sketches on the walls. His artisans began to turn out the 403 *Shawbti* (little statues bearing the implements of labour and usually put in big wooden boxes in the tomb to save the Pharaoh from tedious work in the hereafter). Funerary furniture was designed and made. And since secrecy was vital, only the workers from the city at Deir el Medina (pages 70/71) toiled on the tombs and only the Pharaoh himself and the high priests knew the actual site.

It is probable that the priests actually possessed an architectural plan or blueprint for the construction of tombs in the valley. Though none has ever been found, one cannot believe that a people capable of placing an obelisk of solid granite upright on a small rectangular base, of planning irrigation canals, and, with their obsession for accuracy, of dividing the year—nearly 4000 years B.C.—into 365 days and thus forming the basis of the calendar we use today, that such a people would hazard a guess about that most vital decision: where to dig a Pharaoh's tomb. Admittedly the first corridor of the tomb of Ramses III actually breaks through into another tomb—that of Amen-mesis, one of the pretenders to the throne at the end of the 19th Dynasty—and is consequently diverted and continued to the right. While this might indicate the absence of any blueprint it may equally be the exception that proves the rule.

[1] James Breasted, *The Dawn of Conscience*, Charles Scribner, 1947, p. 100.

What a sad turn of fate that, despite the remoteness of the site, enforced secrecy, complexity of structure and diversion shafts, the tombs were robbed from earliest times! In fact they were probably penetrated soon after they were sealed. Lust for gold, though the main, was not the only reason for their violation. The sacred corridors were also penetrated by enemies of the Pharaoh who wanted to prevent him from continuing his rule in the hereafter. There has been vicious mutilation of some of the mummies. Ramses VI, for example, when unwrapped after having been found hidden in the tomb of Amenhotep II, was discovered to have been literally hacked to pieces.

On the coffins of Seti I and Ramses II are records of a century and a half of persistent effort by the priests to safeguard the royal mummies. Ramses II was first taken from his own tomb to that of his father Seti I. Later he was hidden in the tomb of Queen Inhapi in the shaft at Deir el Bahri. In their haste to rewrap and hide the mummies, the priests sometimes failed to take the necessary precautions; in the wrappings of Ramses I the body of an old lady was found! This was no isolated instance.

As we pass along the corridors of the violated tombs we wonder to what happy stroke of fortune we owe the preservation of one single tomb left almost intact. We wonder why the first robbers of Tutankhamon's tomb—and there are indications that it had been opened and re-sealed — never went back to complete the job. When Ramses VI had his tomb constructed above that of Tutankhamon the rubble undoubtedly fell and obliterated the latter's, but that was over a century later. Whatever the reason, it is thanks to the preservation of the tomb of Tutankhamon that we know the story of the lavish splendour, the artistic merit and the able craftsmanship of the 18th Dynasty.

It is now believed that Tutankhamon's horde, far from being the funerary equipment of one of Egypt's youngest and least significant monarchs, may in fact represent the richest ever buried. Labib Habachi, one of the last survivors of the group of Egyptologists who sorted out the treasures with Howard Carter, feels certain that further study will reveal that a rich heritage from earlier periods was packed into the tiny tomb of the boy-king. Some items so far identified, however, appear to be no more than heirlooms: a statuette of Amenhotep III, a lock of hair from Queen Tiy, a whip of Akhenaten's older brother, a writing-kit of princess Meritaten, and a casket and state fan inscribed with Akhenaten's own name.

## TOMB OF TUTANKHAMON (62): Plan 16

Tutankhamon was the young Pharaoh who succeeded Akhenaten towards the end of the 18th Dynasty. During his nine year rule he restored Thebes as the capital and started the restoration of the worship of Amon. Apart from this all we know of him is that he met a sudden end. Egyptologists did not seem worried that his tomb had never been found. If there were a tomb, they reasoned, it would probably be poor in content. In any case the notable American archeologist Davis had said that the Valley of the Kings had long since yielded all that it had to yield.

Howard Carter, working for Lord Carnarvon, the wealthy Englishman with a passion for ancient Egypt, thought otherwise. He was convinced not only that there was a tomb but that there was a great possibility of its being intact. Carter, in charge of the team, toiled year after year in the desert of the necropolis. For these two, one fruitless year merely built up hope for the next. After six seasons, during which time it was estimated that some 200,000 tons of rubble were moved, Howard Carter was finally forced to accept the fact that his predecessor had probably been right and that the valley had no tomb to yield. It was a depressing decision and one that he could not bring himself to take. For there was one last, very remote possibility: the site immediately beneath the tomb of Ramses VI. It was covered with roughly-constructed workmen's huts. On instructions from Carter his men set about demolishing them.

It was 1922. At the bottom of the steps was the doorway of a tomb. As yet it was too early to tell whose, but the seals seemed intact. Cables were sent to Lord Carnarvon in England while preparations were made for the opening.

Whatever had been expected, or hoped for, there is no doubt that the tomb's actual contents surpassed the wildest dreams. When we gaze at the contents which now lie in Cairo Museum we can almost feel the agony of suspense, exhilaration and utter amazement that must have overwhelmed the first to see the fabulous treasures. The opening was attended by Lord Carnarvon himself who unhappily never lived to see the full richness of the contents of the tomb, as well as by Lady Evelyn Herbert, Professor Breasted and Dr Alan Gardiner.

The tomb proved to be small, but packed to bursting with furniture, emblems, utensils, ornaments, bows, arrows and walking-sticks. Comforts for the Pharaoh in the hereafter included a fly-whisk trimmed with ostrich feathers and a camp-bed folded in three parts. There were necklets, pendants, rings and ear-rings, to say nothing of the shrines and sarcophagi. According to Carter, who spent ten years cataloguing the contents, there were 171 objects in the first room alone. When he had made a small opening in the door of the tomb chamber, he had been faced with what appeared to be a wall of solid gold. It turned out to be an enormous gilded shrine within which, one after another, lay no less than three others. Within these were a stone sarcophagus and three mummy coffins. The one holding the Pharaoh's remains was in solid gold and alone weighed 2,488.8 lbs (1128.9 Kg).

Whilst the world press was focussed on Thebes it was not surprising that one imaginative journalist should attribute the death of Lord Carnarvon to 'The Pharaoh's curse—a sting from a mosquito entombed for centuries'. It added spice to an already fermenting excitement and a growing tourist trade. Vendors and photographers had a heyday in the sacred valley, while forgers were turning out 'antiquities' wholesale.

The mummy was found to be resplendent in gold, with a solid gold mask on the head. There were bracelets, chains, collars, gold beads and necklets of precious and semi-precious stones, engraved *scarabs* and garlands of flowers. Only the outer mummy case, which contains the Pharaoh's mummy, has been left on site. The rest are in the Cairo Museum. But it is as well to bear these treasures in mind as we enter this, the smallest tomb in the Valley of the Kings, for the walls of the first chamber (Plan 16 *A*) which measure a mere eight by four metres, are shockingly bare. Bare, too, are the walls of the small annex (*B*) which contained vessels and containers for oils, baskets of fruit and seed, wine jars and pottery, all decorated in alabaster, ebony, turquoise, gold, lapis-lazuli and ivory.

The only chamber with decorated walls is the burial chamber itself (*C*). The paintings are in almost perfect condition. The religious scenes and inscriptions retain the vivid colour of the day they were painted. There are full-length figures on three of the walls standing beneath a dark band which represents the sky. The wall on the left (*a*) has representations from the Book of the Dead. One is immediately struck by the proportion of the figures, which appear top-heavy. This was of course a characteristic of the Amarna period.

Questions spring to the mind. Why should the walls, apart from the tomb chamber, have been so devoid of decoration when it was believed to be imperative for every stage of the journey to the underworld to be faithfully followed? Why were the contents placed in the disorder indicated in the photographs taken just after the

Tutankhamon's gold-plated outer mummy case.

opening of the tomb? And how could so vast an array of splendid provisions have been completed in the short span of nine years during which the boy-king ruled? Would a young monarch have been anything but sure that time was in his favour?

The provisions for the hereafter can be easily explained. Tutankhamon was the last in the family line and his tomb was filled not merely with his own but with family treasures. Many of the pieces had been taken from the royal temples of Tel el Amarna. The priceless royal throne in Cairo Museum, for example, shows the young king being anointed by his wife against a background of the life-giving Aten, symbol of his father-in-law's heresy. So even though Tutankhamon had completely renounced the teachings of Akhenaten he carried his symbols to his grave. Many of the glazed vases and sceptres clearly originated in the other capital. In addition some of the funerary objects were proved to have been made, not for Tutankhamon, but for Semenkare, Akhenaten's son-in-law and co-regent. These included one of the larger shrines, some of the mummy ornaments and the miniature canopic coffins which had for some reason been usurped and used in Tutankhamon's tomb.

The disorder is undoubtedly indicative of hurry, as is the lack of decoration on the tomb walls. It is clear that the young king met a sudden death and was buried in haste. Murder? Suicide? Until 1969 the mummy revealed no secrets. But the results of an anthropological and skeletal examination of the Pharaoh's mummy, carried out by the Departments of Anatomy of Cairo and Liverpool Universities, are now at hand and it appears that death could have been caused by a blow on the head. Nearly half a century ago Howard Carter had said that there was a 'scab' on the Pharaoh's head. Now Professor Harrison of Liverpool University claims that the unusual thinness of the outer skull of the mummy could have resulted from a haemorrhage beneath the membranes overlying the brain. The X-ray examination has ruled out the theory that Tutankhamon died of tuberculosis.

If the young Pharaoh proves to have been murdered after all, it raises another question. Who was guilty? Was it his tutor Ay, who coveted his young wife and probably married her after Tutankhamon's death? Or was it General Haremhab who had designs on the throne and actually succeeded in seizing it from the blue-bloods at the beginning of the 19th Dynasty?

The Goddess Nephthys spreads protective wings over Tutankhamon's sarcophagus.

# 112

## Plan 17
## TOMB OF SETI I

These tombs have not been drawn to the same scale.
Tutenkhamon's tomb is very small; Seti I's is the largest:

## Plan 16
## TOMB OF TUTENKHAMON

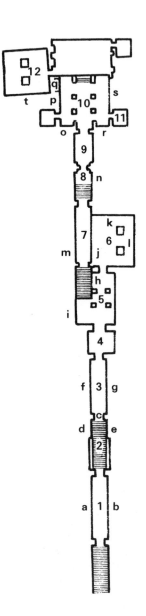

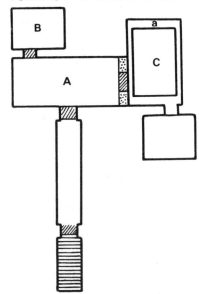

## TOMB OF SETI I (17): Plan 17

Note: *This is a classical tomb that far surpasses all others in the Valley of the Kings both in size and in the artistic execution of the sculptured walls. Every inch of wall space of its entire 100-metre length is covered with representations which were carried out by the finest craftsmen.*

Giovanni Belzoni, who discovered the tomb in 1817, was a circus strong man who originally came to Egypt to market an irrigation pump he had designed in England. The project fell through but he arranged the successful transportation of the colossal head of Ramses II from the Ramasseum to the British Museum in London, and by the standards of the day he was forthwith an archeologist! He turned his energies to the Valley of the Kings and made this remarkable find just one year later. When the Turkish officials in Egypt heard of the discovery they straightway made for the tomb, bent on the delightful thought of acquiring priceless treasure. Down the corridors they went, ransacking every corner only to find to their disappointment that the tomb contained no more than an empty sarcophagus.

A steep flight of stairs leads to the entrance of Seti's tomb which is covered with sacred texts along its full length from the highest reaches down to the bed rock. The first corridor (*1*) is carved in high relief. On the left-hand wall (*a*) the sun-disc bearing a scarab, and the ram-headed Sun-god can be seen between a serpent, a crocodile and two cows' heads. The texts which start on the left are continued to the right (*b*). The roof is painted with flying vultures.

The second corridor (*2*), which is staircased, has thirty-seven forms of the Sun-god depicted on the upper part of the recesses on both sides. As we descend to the third corridor, Maat, goddess of truth, faces us with outstretched wings above the doorway (*c*). Isis is represented on the left-hand side (*d*), and Nephthys on the right (*e*), and they both kneel on the hieroglyph for 'gold' and place their hands upon a seal ring. Above them, on each side of the corridor, the jackal-god Anubis can be seen. The wall reliefs here have not been completed but we can see the outlines in black, the master's touch in red, and the accuracy with which the relief is carved from the bottom upwards.

Proceeding beneath Maat with her outstretched wings we pass into the third corridor (*3*), which has dramatic representations of the fifth hour of night from the fifth chapter of the Book of the Dead. Towards the middle of the left-hand wall (*f*) the sun-boat (damaged) is driven through the netherworld by seven gods and seven goddesses and in front of it march four gods and the goddess Isis. On the right-hand wall (g) the Sun-god and his retinue are drawn through a land inhabited by demons and monsters (top and bottom rows) and we see a serpent with three heads, wings and human legs. But the Sun-god is safe, drawn by Horus and Thoth (middle row) who carry an eye as a protection against evil. The ceiling is blackened from the candles of the early Christians who hid in the tomb.

From the third corridor onwards the quality of the colour on the reliefs is superb. We now come to a small ante-chamber (4). The walls, both to left and right, show the Pharaoh between Harmachis and Isis offering wine to Hathor.

We now enter a square chamber with four pillars (5). On the pillars themselves the Pharaoh is shown before the various deities: Isis and Nephthys the sister-wife and the sister of Osiris, Hathor the goddess of joy and love who was also the goddess of Dendera to whom the cow was sacred, Selket the goddess to whom the scorpion was sacred, Horus the national Sun-god, and Harsiesis and Harmaches who were special forms of Horus; also of course Anubis, the jackal-god of embalming. The walls, especially those at the sides, have marvellous representations of the sun travelling through the fourth region of the underworld. On the rear wall (h) Osiris is enthroned before Hathor while the Pharaoh is led into his presence by the hawk-headed Horus. This is a superb mural with intricate detail and rich colour. Near the corner of the left-hand wall (i) the four chief races of men known at the time stand before Horus: these are Egyptians, Asiatics with pointed beards and coloured aprons, four negroes and four Libyans with feathers on their heads and tattooed bodies.

The chamber (6), situated to the right and entered via a narrow flight of steps, was never completed. Whether this was because it was discovered that the walls were of inferior material, or as a blind to mislead grave-robbers, is not known, but the sketches on the walls are bold and compelling and show the touch of a master craftsman. The original sketch was done in red. The corrections in black were probably the work of the senior artist, after which the carvers took over. The left-hand wall (j) shows the journey during the ninth hour of the underworld: the sacred cow, ram, bird and human head guarding the procession against the fiery serpents. On the rear-wall (k) is the tenth hour with the hawk joining the protective deities and the spirits carrying arrows and lances. On the right-hand wall (l) is

Astrological figures on the roof of the burial chamber of Seti I's Tomb.

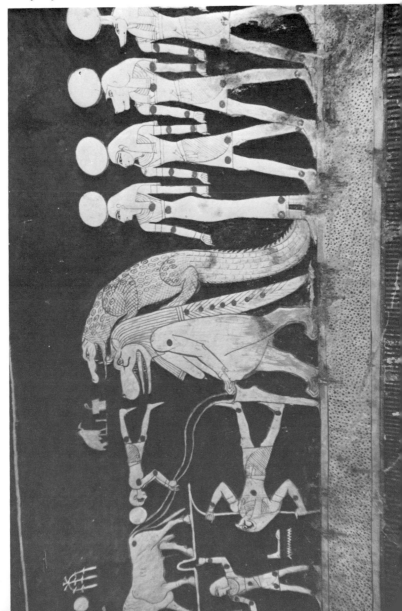

the eleventh hour with the condemned in the lower row. The enemies of the Sun-god are being burned under the supervision of the hawk-headed Horus in strange furnaces, whilst fire-breathing goddesses stand watch with swords.

We retrace our steps to the chamber of pillars (*5*), to the left of which a stairway, carefully concealed by the builders of the tomb, descends to the fourth corridor (*7*). To the left of this corridor (*m*) is a figure of the Pharaoh (destroyed) seated at an offering table. Above him hovers a hawk and before him stands a priest.

We descend a few more steps into a small corridor (*8*) which is decorated with texts of the ceremonies performed before the statue of the deceased Pharaoh in order that he may eat and drink in the hereafter. On the right-hand wall (*n*) is a list of offerings.

The ante-chamber (*9*) is decorated with the gods of the dead including Anubis, Isis, Hathor, Harsiesis and Osiris. Finally we come to a large hall (*10*). Here a slight incline with steps at the sides takes us to the burial chamber, which comprises two portions. The front portion has pillars and the rear portion a vaulted ceiling. It was in the rear section that the alabaster sarcophagus of the Pharaoh stood when the tomb was discovered. It was made out of a single piece of alabaster, carved to a thickness of two inches and with the exquisite reliefs filled in with blue paste. This magnificent piece is comparable only to the alabaster vase found in Tutankhamon's tomb which is today in the Cairo Museum. The mummy, which was one of those found at Deir el Bahri, is in the same museum. The sarcophagus lies in the Soane Museum in London. When Belzoni effected its transportation to England, the Trustees of the British Museum considered the price set too high and the treasure was without a buyer until 1824 when Sir John Soane paid Henry Salt £2,000 for it.

The decorations on the walls of the pillared portion of the hall show the journey through the first region of the underworld on the left entrance-wall (*o*) and through the fourth region of the underworld on the left-hand wall (*p*). In a small recess at the end of this wall (*q*) is a beautiful representation of Anubis performing the opening-of-the-mouth ceremony before Osiris. On the right-hand entrance wall (*r*) and the right-hand wall (*s*) are representations of the journey through the second region of the underworld.

The vaulted ceiling has been painted with astrological figures. From early times, of course, the Egyptians had mapped out the heavens, identified some of the fixed stars and were able to determine the positions of others. This ceiling is unusual in that it has not

Unfinished relief work in the Tomb of Seti I (Chamber 6).

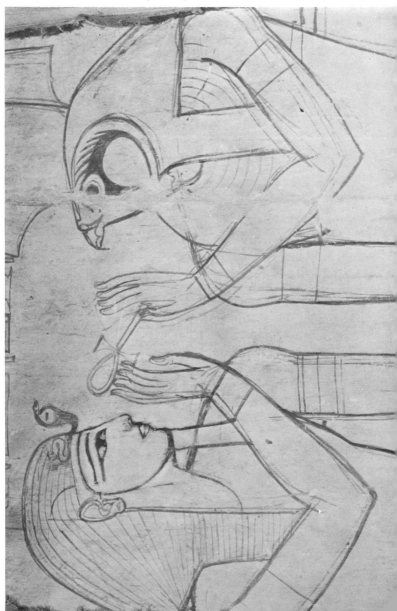

been painted in the familiar balanced, repetitive form.

Adjoining the tomb chamber are four side-rooms. The first one on the right (*11*) has the text of a myth that concerns the rebellion of mankind against the Sun-god, their punishment and final rescue. On the rear wall is a magnificent relief of the heavenly cow of the myth supported by Shu, the god of the atmosphere, and bearing on its back two boats of the sun.

The chamber on the left (*12*) has a shelf decorated with a cornice running round the three main walls. It contains more dramatic representations of the Pharaoh's progress through various provinces, safeguarded by the spells of Isis, the sacred ibis and the ostrich feather—symbol of justice and truth. Spirits and demons (left-hand wall (*t*), middle row) greet the procession. The foes of Osiris are beheaded by a lion-headed god (top row), and dwellings of the deceased gods and spirits open their doors as the Sun-god approaches (rear wall (*u*), middle row), showing the dead restored to life, and serpents with heads of genii of the dead upon their backs, or with swords in their hands, rising in unison to annihilate the foes of the Sun-god at the end of the journey.

The Pharaoh will overcome. With the help of the Sun-god the doors of the hereafter are open to him. He will enter with his valuables and possessions; with the ability to eat and drink; and imbued with life so as to reign again.

This is his ultimate hope.

Some fifteen years ago Sheikh Abdel Rasool, a descendant of the Rasool family of Deir el Bahri fame, told the Antiquities Department that he considered it his duty to share with them an intelligence that had come down by word of mouth for generations: that beyond the burial chamber in the tomb of Seti I was another chamber.

Although such an extension beyond the burial chamber would be completely irregular, excavations were nevertheless enthusiastically commenced in the hope that if there were such a chamber it would contain some of the funerary furniture of the deceased. The passage was cleared and continued on a steep decline. The walls bore no decoration. Nearly ninety metres were dug before work was to be abandoned when it was noticed that fissures had appeared in the burial chamber, doubtless caused by the vibration, temperature and humidity changes from the workers.

Although excavations were halted, visitors were not. All were intent on seeing the largest, most beautifully decorated and well

A scene from the burial chamber of Ramses VI.

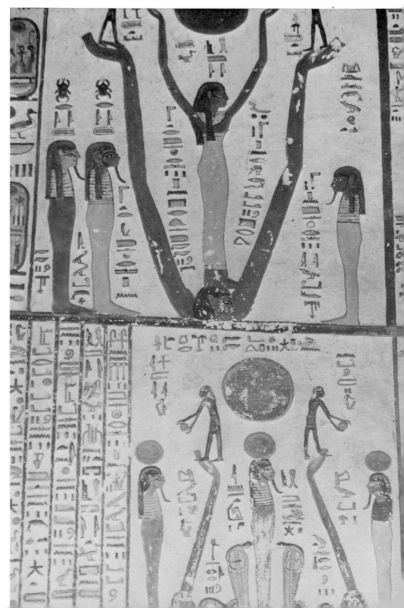

preserved tomb in the Valley of the Kings. Sometimes groups of tourists would overlap, adding to the humidity. There would be jostling in the corridors, with people pressing against the unprotected reliefs. For some reason countless tourists trail their fingers, often damp from the heat, along the outlines of carvings. Little wonder that such abuse should take its toll. Seti's tomb became a victim of tourism and was closed for several years to prevent further damage. (See Chapter 10 'A Plea for Luxor'.)

## TOMB OF AMENHOTEP II (35): Plan 18

This tomb was excavated in 1898. The attention of Loret, the prominent French archeologist, was drawn to it by local *felaheen*. It was a remarkable find. For one thing it was the first tomb ever opened in which the Pharaoh was found where he had been laid. Secondly, there was a windfall of mummies in a sealed-off chamber, including nine of royalty. Thirdly, the burial chamber proved to be one of the most beautiful, certainly the most original, in the entire Valley of the Kings. But more important, the tomb was nearly complete and contained a complete and unspoiled set of texts from the Book of the Dead.

The first corridors are rough and undecorated. They lead to a shaft (now bridged), a false burial chamber (*1*) created to confuse robbers, and finally to the actual tomb chamber (*2*). This is supported by six pillars and the sarcophagus of the Pharaoh lay in the crypt-like section at the rear. The mummy was festooned and garlanded and the sandstone sarcophagus was all that the grave-robbers had left. Everything else had been ruthlessly plundered.

As one enters the tomb chamber one is immediately struck by the originality and beauty of the decorations. The figures on the columns—for the most part depicting Amenhotep and the gods of the underworld—are outlined in black with only his crown, jewellery, belt and the surrounding decorations in colour. The drawing is exquisitely fine and the blue roof is covered with stars. The walls are painted yellow and the traditional religious formulae are so drawn as to give the impression of papyrus texts having been pinned to the walls. There is not too much detail and the use of the pigment is beneficially restrained. As already explained, the Book of the Dead was a development of the magical formulae inscribed on the inside of the coffins of the Middle Kingdom. With the aid of these formulae the deceased would overcome the foes to his eternal triumph in the underworld. Only with the magic inscriptions

From the Book of the Dead, Tomb of Ramses VI.

could he hope to make his heart (conscience) acceptable in the awesome presence of Osiris when it was weighed against the feather of truth; and only thus could he hope to live securely forever.

On each side of the chamber are two small rooms. Three mummies lay in the first to the right (*3*), and in the second (*4*) were nine royal mummies including Thutmose IV, Amenhotep III, Seti II and Ramses IV, V and VI. All have been taken to Cairo Museum. Not surprisingly this quickly became known as the *Safety Tomb* and this is undoubtedly what the priests had intended it for. When they found that Amenhotep II's tomb had been violated they reasoned that the robbers would not return to its ravaged corridors. In fact they never did. The royal personages remained in peace for centuries.

When Loret excavated the tomb quite a controversy arose as to whether the mummy should be left on site or whether it should be removed with the others to the museum. It was finally agreed that it should remain on site but with an armed guard. Nearly three years later the tomb was rifled when, deliberately or otherwise, the backs of the guards were turned. The mummy of Amenhotep was found

## TOMB OF AMENHOTEP II  Plan 18

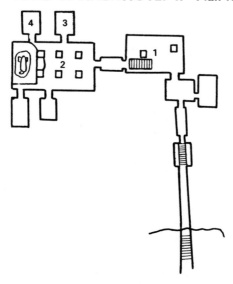

Burial Chamber of the Tomb of Amenhotep II.

on the floor, in a very much poorer condition as a result of delving and prying hands in search of overlooked treasures in the folds of the cloth. There was now no question about it. The mummy of the Pharaoh was placed in Cairo Museum. The marvellous sandstone sarcophagus stands on site.

## TOMB OF RAMSES VI (9): Plan 19

This tomb was started by Ramses V and was usurped by his successor. It has three entrance halls, two chambers, a further two corridors, an ante-chamber and the tomb chamber. The wall representations are carried out in low painted relief. The standard of craftsmanship is not high but the tomb chamber itself has one of the most important ceilings in the Valley of the Kings. In fact names and mottoes in Coptic and Greek show that this *Golden Hall* was an attraction from the first century A.D.

The first three corridors carry texts and representations from the Praises of Ra. On both sides of the first corridor, at (*a*) and (*b*), the deceased Pharaoh stands before the deities Harakhte and Osiris. On the right-hand side of the second corridor (*c*) is the barge of the Sun-god with the twelve hours of night. Towards the end of the left-hand wall (*d*) is the figure of Osiris before whom is the boat of the Sun-god. A pig (representing evil) is being driven away from it by sacred dog-headed apes. We now pass into the third corridor.

On the roof there is a painting of the goddess Nut which extends from the beginning of the corridor (*3*), through the ante-chamber (*4*) where her body curves to the right of the roof, and ends in the chamber (*5*). On the right-hand wall of the third corridor is a superb representation of Osiris under a canopy (*e*).

The chamber (*5*) has four columns and a sloping passage at the rear which is guarded by sacred winged snakes. The columns show the Pharaoh making offerings to the deities. The roof is rich in colour. On the rear walls (*f*) and (*g*) are representations of the enthroned Osiris before whom the deceased burns incense. Though the colour is well-preserved, the reliefs are inferior when compared to those in the tomb of Seti I.

The following corridor (*6*) takes us further along the road to the underworld. On the left-hand side (*h*) is the journey in the fourth hour with the sacred cow (centre row) and the crocodile in a boat (second row).

The sloping corridor (*7*) has sacred and protective emblems and religious formulae from the book of 'That which is in the Under-

**TOMB OF RAMSES VI**

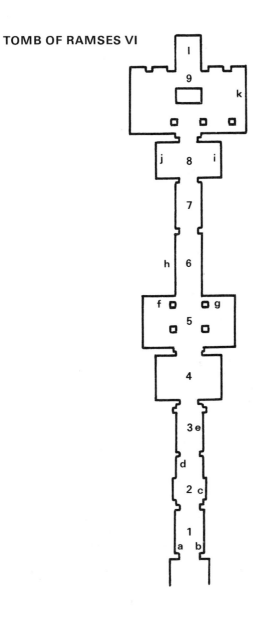

world', and leads to an ante-chamber (*8*). On the right-hand wall (*i*) is the deceased Pharaoh with Maat. The left-hand wall (*j*) has texts from the Book of the Dead.

Dark blue and gold predominate in the tomb chamber (*9*). Across the vaulted ceiling the goddess Nut is twice represented along its entire length, in a graceful semi-circle with backs touching. This represents the morning and evening skies. Her elongated body curves to touch the earth with finger and toe, head to the west, loins to the east.

The entire chamber is a complex of appropriate texts from the Book of the Dead. For example, on the right-hand wall (*k*) is a small representation (second row) of the boat of the Sun-god, who is represented in the shape of a beetle with a ram's head. The boat is being worshipped by two human-headed birds and the souls of Kheper and Atum (forms of the Sun-god). Below this scene (to left and right) are the beheaded condemned and above is a representation of the goddess Nut with upstretched arms.

In the niche at the rear of the tomb chamber (*l*) is the barge of the Sun-god held aloft in upstretched arms.

The smashed sarcophagus of the Pharaoh was left on site by the grave-robbers and priests restored the damaged mummy, which was found in 1898 in the tomb of Amenhotep II.

## TOMB OF RAMSES III (11): Plan 20

This tomb is second in size only to that of Seti I and has become known as the *Tomb of the Harpists*. Its construction differs from the regular tomb in that five small chambers lead off either side of the first and second corridors, making ten in all. Each is devoted to aspects of the Pharaoh's life. It is also interesting that the first part of the tomb — up to the third room — was built by Setnakht, father of Ramses III, and in places where the paint has fallen off his cartouches are revealed. This is the tomb, it will be remembered, where the third corridor was diverted to the right after its builders had broken into an adjacent tomb by mistake (see page 105).

Although the wall decorations may not be considered of the best artistic quality, their variety and richness are certainly unsurpassed. The entrance door is at the foot of a flight of steps on each side of which are small pillars with bulls' heads. Over the door is a representation of Isis and Nephthys worshipping the sun-disc. Along the first corridor are figures of Maat, goddess of integrity and truth, kneeling and sheltering with her wings the deceased Pharaoh as his body enters the tomb. On the walls are Praises of Ra. The Pharaoh himself can be seen on the left-hand wall before Harmaches (one of the forms of the Sun-god), followed by the familiar sacred serpent, crocodile and two gazelles' heads.

We now turn to the five small chambers leading off the *left-hand side* of the corridor. The first chamber (*a*) contains various scenes of cooking, slaughtering and baking. The second chamber (*b*) has, on the entrance wall to the left, the kneeling god of the Nile bestowing his gifts to seven gods of fertility which have ears of corn on their heads. On the wall to the right the Nile-god is seen before the serpent-headed goddess Napret, five apron-clad royal snakes and two gods of fertility. The third chamber (*c*) is largely decorated with male and female local deities with offerings. In the bottom row are kneeling Nile-gods. The fourth chamber (*d*) has representations of the guardian spirit of the deceased on either side of the entrance, each bearing a staff ending in a royal head. The other walls show double rows of rowers, sacred serpents and sacred cattle. The fifth chamber (*e*) contains the representations that gave the tomb its name: on the left wall are two harpists, one before Anhor and the hawk-headed Harmaches, and the other before Shu and Atum. The text on either side of the doorway is the song they sing asking that the blessed Pharaoh might be received.

As already stated, there are five chambers on the *right-hand side* of the corridor. The first (*f*) contains a double row of sailing ships: those in the upper row ready to set sail and those in the lower with sails furled. The second chamber (*g*) is the Pharaoh's armoury. The walls have representations of all the royal weapons and standards. At the top of the left-hand wall are standards with heads of sacred animals. At the top of the right-hand wall are standards with gods' heads. On the rear wall are a multitude of bows, arrows and quivers. The third chamber (*h*) is particularly interesting if we remember that this was a very wealthy Pharaoh, for it contains his treasury. On the walls are representations of furniture and ornaments, utensils and jewellery, elaborate head-rests, cushioned benches and comfortable couches that are attained by steps. The fourth chamber (*i*) has rural scenes. The Pharaoh sails along a canal watching ploughing, sowing and reaping. In the fields are sacred animals. The last chamber on the right-hand side (*j*) is notable for its twelve different forms of Osiris, the god of the underworld.

The fourth corridor is decorated with scenes from the Book of the Dead, and leads to an ante-chamber (*5*) with representations of the Pharaoh in the presence of the gods of the underworld. The sloping

# 128

**TOMB OF RAMSES III**

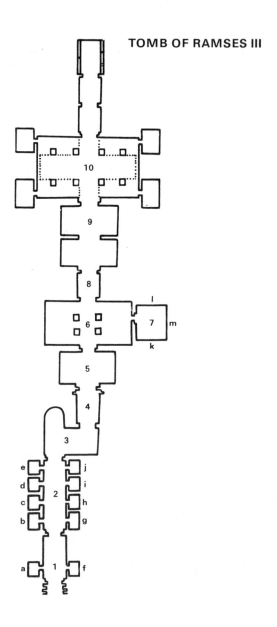

passage (6) that follows has side galleries supported by four pillars, and a doorway on the right leading to a small chamber (7); here are some fine representations: on the right-hand wall (k) the Pharaoh is guided by the deities Thoth and Har-Khentkheti. On the left-hand wall (l) he presents the image of truth to Osiris, god of the underworld. On the rear wall (m) the Pharaoh stands in the presence of Osiris.

The following corridor (8) is badly damaged, as are the ante-chambers that precede the tomb chamber itself (10). This is a long oblong room with four pillars on each side and an extra chamber at each of the four corners. The actual sarcophagus is now in the Louvre, its lid is in Cambridge, and the Pharaoh's mummy, amongst those taken from the shaft at Deir el Bahri, is now in the Cairo Museum.

## TOMB OF RAMSES IX (6): Plan 21

This tomb is constructed on fairly classical lines and comprises three chambers, one following the other in a straight line. It is approached by an inclined plane with steps on either side. Flanking the doorway are representations of the deceased standing before Harmaches and Osiris (a), and Amon and a goddess of the dead (b). The two pairs of chambers in this part of the corridor have no decorations.

On the right-hand wall, over the second chamber on the right (c) are demons of the underworld including serpents and ghosts with the heads of bulls and jackals. At this point is the beginning of the text of the sun's journey through the underworld. On the left-hand side of the corridor (d) a priest pours forth the symbols for life, wealth, etc. on the deceased Pharaoh, who is dressed like Osiris. The priest wears the side-lock of a royal prince and is probably a son of the deceased.

The roof of the second corridor (2) is decorated with constellations. To both left and right (e) serpents rear themselves. Note the recesses for figures of the gods, followed on the left-hand wall (f) with the beginning of another text from the Book of the Dead and the deceased Pharaoh before the hawk-headed Sun-god. On the opposite wall (g) are demons and spirits.

The third corridor (3) is also protected by serpents. On the right-hand wall (h) the Pharaoh presents an image of Maat to Ptah, the god of Memphis, beside whom stands the goddess Maat. Note that the transparent cloth of the skirt is carved deeply thus enabling the foot and front legs of the Pharaoh to appear in low relief. Immediately beyond this representation we see the mummy of the Pharaoh across a mountain, symbolising the resurrection. The *scarab* and the sun-disc (above) indicate the bringing forth of renewed life on the earth. Towards the middle of this same wall (at

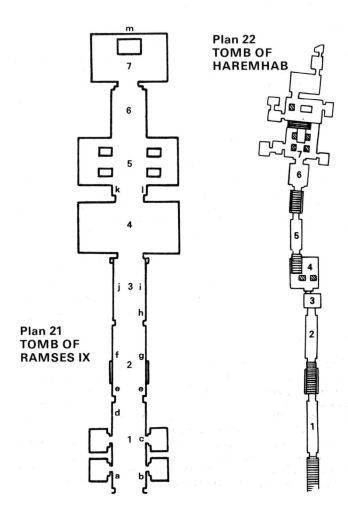

**Plan 22**
**TOMB OF**
**HAREMHAB**

**Plan 21**
**TOMB OF**
**RAMSES IX**

*i*) are ritualistic representations including four men spitting out *scarabs* as they bend over backwards, demons standing upon serpents, serpents pierced by arrows and the *scarab* in a boat with two Horus eyes.

On the left-hand wall (*j*) are the boats of the Sun-god (centre) travelling through the second and third hours of night bearing protective divinities.

We now enter a chamber (*4*). Beyond, at (*k*) and (*l*), are priests with panther skins and side-locks, sacrificing and making offerings before a standard. The next chamber (*5*) is rough and unfinished and slopes downwards to the burial chamber through another corridor (*6*). In the burial chamber (*7*) there are traces (on the floor) of the sarcophagus. On the walls are gods and demons. The goddess Nut, representing the morning and evening skies, is shown across the rough ceiling in two figures. Below are constellations, boats of the stars, etc. On the rear wall (*m*) the child Horus, seated within the winged sun-disc, is symbolic of rebirth after death.

## TOMB OF HAREMHAB (57): Plan 22

This tomb, which was plundered in antiquity, has an unimpressive entrance with steps through two corridors and is followed by the *well-room* (*3*) and by a hall (*4*) that was completed to resemble the tomb chamber. The stairway on the left-hand side of this hall, though carefully concealed, was nevertheless found by robbers who, following the corridor (*5*), passed through the ante-chamber (*6*) and plundered the tomb chamber (*7*).

This tomb is worth a visit for four reasons. First for the extremely high quality of the reliefs of the well-room (*3*) and the ante-chamber (*6*). Secondly, to see the stages of mural execution in some of the corridors where the work has not been completed and especially in the burial chamber (*7*). Thirdly, because in the six-pillared burial hall the sarcophagus is a fine piece of work in red granite with beautifully carved figures of the various deities along with the religious formulae. At the corners goddesses spread their wings to guard the deceased. Their protection was inadequate, for when the American archeologist Davis excavated the tomb in 1905 the mummy was in such poor condition as even to prevent confirmation of its sex. Fourthly, because on the higher reaches of the tomb chamber are the symbols for north, south, east and west and it is interesting to observe that these were instructions for the workers, who were given appropriate decorations for each.

## TOMB OF THUTMOSE III (34): Plan 23

This is the tomb of the world's first empire builder. A steep flight of stairs across a dramatic ravine between sheer mountain faces leads to the remote entrance. It was excavated in the 18th Dynasty when the Pharaoh's chief aim was concealment. When it became evident that these precautions were useless, the tombs of the 19th Dynasty were grouped together under an armed guard.

The design is simple. After the stairway a sloping corridor descends to a staircase which has broad niches on both sides (*1*). Beyond this is another corridor leading to a rectangular shaft (crossed by a hand-bridge) and into a chamber (*2*) which has two undecorated pillars and a ceiling covered with stars. The walls bear the names of 741 different deities.

The tomb chamber (*3*) is approached by a stairway and is in the form of an oval. The scenes of the underworld are mostly in excellent condition. The representations on the pillars are delightfully simplified black drawings. On the face of the first is a religious inscription and on the left-hand face (from top to bottom) are Thutmose and his queen-mother Isis in a boat, the king being suckled by Isis in the form of a tree and (below) the king being followed by his three wives and the princess Nofretere. On the third face of the pillar are demons. Demons and religious inscriptions adorn the other pillars. The sarcophagus, on an alabaster pedestal, was made of red sandstone and was found to be empty. The Pharaoh's mummy was safely in the Deir el Bahri shaft.

**Plan 23**

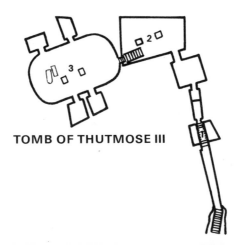

**TOMB OF THUTMOSE III**

# CHAPTER 7   THE NECROPOLIS
# THE VALLEY OF THE QUEENS

## BACKGROUND

In this valley by no means all the queens of the New Kingdom were buried. It appears that a special burial ground for the royal consorts was started only in the reign of Ramses I and royal offspring were also buried here. There are signs that previously the queens were laid to rest beside their husbands in the Valley of the Kings, but pillage of the royal tombs makes it difficult to confirm this.

There are over twenty tombs in the Valley of the Queens. Many are unfinished and entirely without decoration, resembling caves rather than sacred tomb chambers. The most impressive is that of the wife of Ramses II, Queen Nefer-tari, his favourite. Although her tomb is officially closed, it will nevertheless be described to give a picture of the memorial to a Pharaoh's love. (The French Association for Artistic Action donated the profits of the 1979 exhibition of the relics of Ramses II in Paris, to the Egyptian Government for restoration of the funeral chamber of Nefer-tari's tomb.)

## TOMB OF NEFER-TARI (66): Plan 24

Nefer-tari or 'Beautiful Companion' has a magnificent tomb comprising an entrance hall (*1*) with a side chamber (*2*) leading off to the right. A corridor stairway (*3*) leads to the burial chamber (*4*) which has four square pillars and, in the centre, a few stairs leading to what was once the site of the sarcophagus, sunk slightly lower than the ground rock. The walls throughout the tomb are elaborately worked in low relief, partly filled with stucco and painted.

The first thing that strikes one on entry into the tomb is the extravagant use of colour and its astounding brilliance. The flesh hues, white robes, black hair, bright friezes give the impression of having been newly painted. And the second thing is the realism with which the queen herself has been painted. She is graceful and sensitive and extremely beautiful. Her form, as she appears before the various deities, is accompanied by only a modest amount of text. This, despite the excessive detail of the drawings, gives the im-

# I34

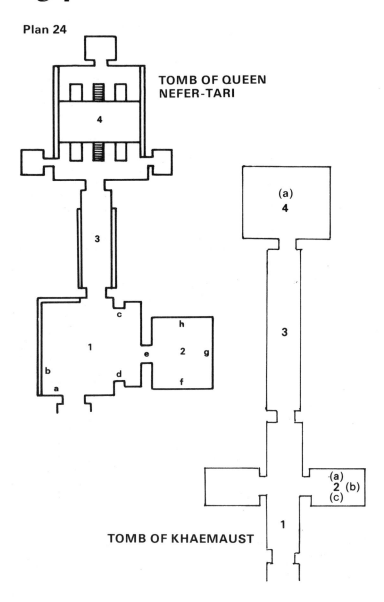

Plan 24

TOMB OF QUEEN NEFER-TARI

4

3

c

h

1

2

g

e

b

a

d

f

TOMB OF KHAEMAUST

(a)
4

3

(a)
2 (b)
(c)

1

pression of simplification, somewhat as though the presence of one so beautiful spoke for itself.

On the left-hand wall of the first chamber (*a*) is a series of magical formulae with the queen playing at a board game. At (*b*) the *ka* worships the rising sun between two lions which symbolise the immediate past and the immediate future. To the right at (*c*) and (*d*) the goddesses Neith and Selket receive the queen. Maat, goddess of truth, is represented at each side of the entrance to the annex (*e*).

In the side chamber (*2*) on the right-hand wall (*f*) the queen adores seven sacred cows, the bull and four steering oars of the sky. On the facing wall (*g*) she makes offerings to Osiris (on the left) and Atum (on the right). On the left-hand wall (*h*) she stands before the ibis-headed Thoth while Heket the frog squats before him.

In the staircased corridor (*3*) Nefer-tari makes offerings to Isis (on the left) and Hathor (on the right) while guardian deities protect and guide her.

The murals of the tomb chamber (*4*) are not in such perfect condition but represent the deceased queen again with the deities.

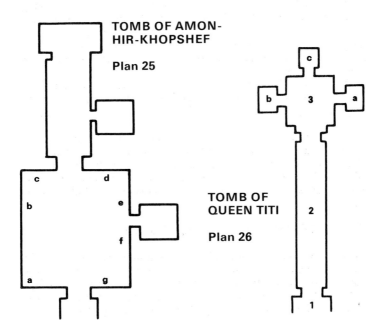

TOMB OF AMON-
HIR-KHOPSHEF

Plan 25

TOMB OF
QUEEN TITI

Plan 26

As usual, demons guard the gates of the underworld and the queen passes by with the aid of the sacred formulae and emblems. In this tomb the safeguards and warnings against evil, and examples of possible sufferings to those not pure in heart, seem to have been used to the minimum. One is conscious of a path of purity through the underworld, as though the journey of Ramses II's beloved was a mere formality.

## TOMB OF AMON-HIR-KHOPSHEF (55): Plan 25

In this charming tomb Ramses III himself leads his son Amon-hir-khopshef into the presence of the divine gods of the underworld. The nine-year-old boy wears the side-lock of youth and carries the feather of truth as he obediently follows his father. The reliefs are of fine quality painted low relief, in excellently preserved colour. In fact the murals of this tomb are amongst the finest on the necropolis.

The tomb comprises a large entrance hall with an unfinished annex to the right and the tomb chamber (unfinished).

On the left-hand wall, travelling clockwise, we see the young prince following the Pharaoh Ramses III, who offers incense to Ptah (a) and then introduces his son. Afterwards he presents the boy to Duamutef and to Imseti (b), who conducts the pair to Isis. Note that Isis (c) looks over her shoulder to the advancing Pharaoh. She holds him by the hand.

On the right-hand wall (continuing clockwise) Ramses and his son are conducted to Hathor (d), Hapi, Kebhsnewef (e) Shu (f) and Nephthys (g) who puts her hand beneath the chin of the bereaved Pharaoh.

The corridors bear scenes from the Book of the Dead.

There was no mummy of the boy in the sarcophagus but in its place was a foetus of six months' development. Perhaps the mother miscarried due to grief at the loss of the boy. One can only speculate. The foetus is preserved in a small hermetically sealed glass in the tomb.

## TOMB OF KHAEMAUST (44): Plan 24

This tomb, which is situated at the southeastern corner of the Valley, at the end of a narrow pathway, belongs to another son of Ramses III. He too died too young to pass into the presence of the gods of the underworld unaccompanied and it is Ramses who introduces him to them. The tomb was never completed and some of the undecorated white plaster coating can be seen.

The first corridor (*1*) is decorated on both sides with representations of the king introducing his son to the different gods and goddesses. It is in the two side chambers, however, that we find the most interesting scenes. Since they are similarly decorated, only one will be described. In the right-hand chamber (*2*), on either side of the doorway, are the goddesses Isis and Nephthys on one side, and Neith and Selket on the other. Moving clockwise, the left-hand wall (*a*) shows the young prince standing alone adoring four demi-gods in turn. The first one is Hapi the Nile-god who has been given a jackal head by mistake! On the rear wall (*b*) Isis and Nephthys talk to two seated figures of Osiris on behalf of the prince. On the right-hand wall (*c*) the prince worships four more demi-gods; Duamutef has here been given the head of an ape instead of a jackal!

The long corridor (*3*), which is vaulted and decorated with scenes to right and left, once again shows Ramses introducing his son to demi-gods. In the rear chamber, however, Ramses III stands alone before the gods interceding for his son.

The rear wall (*d*) repeats the scenes of the four goddesses addressing Osiris. Selket and Nephthys to the right, Isis and Neith to the left. From a lotus flower in front of Osiris, four genii arise.

## TOMB OF QUEEN TITI (52): Plan 26

This is not Queen Tiy, consort of Amenhotep III and mother of Akhenaten, but a queen of the Ramesside era. The tomb is damaged but some of the murals still retain startling freshness of colour. The figures of the gods and demons in the tomb chamber defy the years with their brightness.

The tomb is simple, comprising an ante-chamber (*1*), a long passage (*2*) and the tomb chamber (*3*), which is flanked by three small chambers.

On the rear wall of the chamber flanking the tomb chamber to the right (*a*) is a representation of Hathor who appears in the form of a cow in a mountainous landscape. In front there is a sycamore from which Hathor, now represented in human form, pours out Nile water to revive the queen.

The chamber on the opposite side (*b*) contains the mummy shaft. The rear chamber (*c*) shows genii of the dead and various gods seated at offering tables while the queen prays to them (to left and right). On the rear wall Osiris sits enthroned with Neith and Selket before him and Nephthys, Isis and Thoth behind him.

# 138

## TOMBS OF THE NOBLES
## SHEIKH ABD EL KURNA

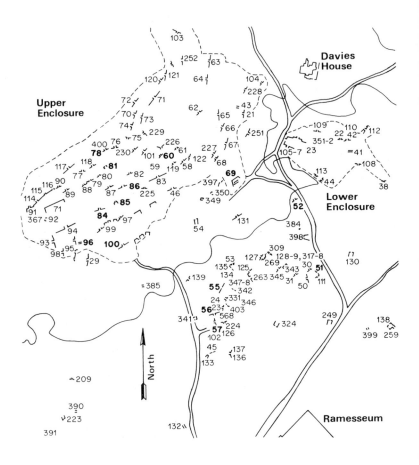

# CHAPTER 8   THE NECROPOLIS
# THE TOMBS OF THE NOBLES

## BACKGROUND

The tombs of the Nobles spread over an area of about two square miles from Dra Abu el Naga in the north to Deir el Medina in the south. There are well over four hundred. All belong to the officials who wielded power, to a greater or lesser extent, in the New Kingdom.

Who were these people, these aristocrats of the age? Perhaps their position is best understood by stressing first of all that the Pharaoh of Egypt was no mere figurehead. His position was supreme and he took an active part in all affairs of state. He was concerned with matters ranging from the height the water rose during the inundation of the Nile in any year, to the recruitment of troops, whom he personally led into battle. He participated in public ceremonies and dedications, supervised the planning and construction of an edifice or a state thoroughfare and even had the final say in the judgement of a petty crime. It can be readily appreciated therefore that this was far too much for a single pair of hands and the Pharaoh's vizier took a share of the responsibility. Along with the chief treasurer, he headed the main government departments. The vizier provided the liaison between the departmental heads and the Pharaoh, just as the departmental heads provided the liaison between the workers and the vizier. In Thebes all the affairs of the state capital filtered through the hands of the vizier before coming to the attention of the Pharaoh, including the annual taxation from officials and recording of tributes from conquered lands.

The viziers held a powerful position and the growth of this power can be traced in their tombs from the days of Thutmose III, when the monarch could afford to be liberal with his loyal and trusted subordinates, giving them gifts and honours in recognition of their services, to the era following Akhenaten's breakaway government when the vizier became the power behind the throne and, taking advantage of a weakening line of monarchs, ultimately gained the supreme position for himself.

These then are the tombs of the grand vizier and of those under his control: the army general, the superintendent of granaries, the overseer of gardens, the scribe of the fields, etc. The majority of tombs were uniform and simple, designed in two parts. There was a wide open court leading to a hall which was sometimes supported by pillars or columns. Directly centre-back of this hall was a long corridor leading to the offering shrine which had niches for the statues of the relatives of the deceased. The walls, due to the poor quality limestone rock, were covered with a layer of clay and then a coat of whitewash. These were painted. There are sculptured reliefs on only a few. The walls of the main hall usually bore prayers for the deceased to the right and a record of his career to the left. The back corridor usually carried the various funerary rites.

The tombs of the nobles differed from those of the Pharaoh in one important respect. Whereas the royal tombs were only burial places, the tombs of the nobles were funerary rooms and burial places combined. The Pharaoh was divine and joy and plenty were automatically assured to him in the hereafter, while a nobleman depicted on the walls of his tomb every aspect of his experience on earth that he wanted repeated in the hereafter. Naturally he chose the most pleasant memories: the perfect harvest, the perfect feast, the perfect catch on the hook and the perfect fowl brought down with an arrow. The happiest hours of his life were captured for the hereafter, the greatest joys and naturally the most praiseworthy honours bestowed on him for his administrative excellence.

These tombs shed a flood of light on the life and times. They are valuable chapters in ancient history. Just as the Sakkara *mastabas* tell us about life in the Old Kingdom and the rock-hewn tombs of Beni Hassan give an insight into the Middle Kingdom, it is the tombs of the nobles that tell us most about the New Kingdom. We see how the people lived, worked, built, fished, speared. We see them enjoying a social function and grieving at a funeral. We see the impassive faces of officials at a public ceremony and the light-hearted gaiety of a group of dancers. In fact here is a new type of art.

Egyptian art, as we have seen, was both religious and idealised, conforming to a strict pattern in the portrayal of the Pharaoh, the deities, battles and festivities. The side-view face was considered more typical of the individual than front-view, whilst front-view eyes were necessary for expression. A side-view of the arms necessarily meant concealing one of them, therefore square shoulders were necessary. Groups of people were shown as parallel outlines behind the front figure. These traditions were never questioned by the state artists and they continued the repetitive positions and positioning from generation to generation. Movement was rare.

In the tombs of the nobles we come across a severe break with these traditions. All the paintings are characterised by naturalism. First of all, in place of the frieze, each wall is surrounded by a decorative border and within each frame is a picture, complete in itself. The outer figures face inwards, movements and actions are varied. There is balance, perspective and, surprisingly, even front-view faces and side-view shoulders. The most delightful drawings are such realistic portrayals as a thirsty man and a naughty child. The natural wit and spontaneity of the artist has at last been released. While national and mortuary temples were normally filled with stylized, grand, heroic and repetitive themes, the walls of the tombs of the nobles were covered with a rich and exciting catalogue of the lives of men, each of whom was a pivot of at least one administrative unit of his time—and not, as sometimes claimed, by cheap substitutes for wall relief.

**TOMB OF NAKHT**

**Plan 27**

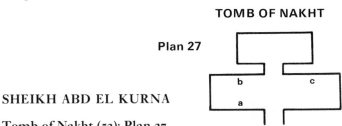

## SHEIKH ABD EL KURNA

### Tomb of Nakht (52): Plan 27

This is the simple tomb of the scribe of the granaries under Thutmose IV. It comprises two chambers and only the first is decorated. But in this single room are such detailed activities, executed with such infinite charm and in such a good state of repair that the tomb of Nakht will always rank as one of the finest. The more detailed the earthly activities depicted in the tomb, the easier for them to be repeated in the hereafter; that much is clear. But this tomb has, in addition, extraordinary and remarkable irrelevances that both surprise and charm.

We will turn to the left after we enter the doorway. On the first wall (*a*) is a series of agricultural scenes including ploughing, digging, sowing, etc. In the upper row the deceased superintends three stages of the harvest: the measuring and winnowing of the grain, the reaping and pressing of the grain into baskets—with a charming drawing of a man leaping in the air so that the weight of his body might press the grain tightly — and, in the lower row, the labourers being organised by the deceased for ploughing in two teams. Note that the ploughman has ragged hair, the ox is piebald and that, in the midst of the strenuous work one of the workers takes a moment's respite to drink from a wineskin on a tree.

On the rear left-hand wall (b) there is a delightful scene showing the deceased and his wife (in the lower row) being brought flowers and geese by their son whilst three women play music to them. These female musicians are sensitively painted in perfect detail. The graceful nude lute-player dances to the accompaniment of a no less graceful flautist and harpist. The body of the one girl is given front-view treatment while her head is turned to speak to her colleague. Above is a blind harpist playing to guests and attended by an audience of women seated on the ground, who are apparently more interested in local gossip than in watching the dancers, and a naked young girl leaning to put perfume before the nostrils of three women. Below Nakht's chair is a bristling cat who has just stolen a feast.

On the right-hand rear wall (c) the deceased is seated with his wife in an arbour (lower row), while flowers, poultry, grapes and fish are brought to them by their servants. Servants were of course a regular feature in the homes of Egypt's noblemen. Each had a specific chore: cleaning the bed-chamber, washing the laundry, acting as nanny.

On this same wall (c) birds are being caught in nets and plucked. The filled net is a complex of wings and colours. Grapes are being picked and turned into wine (lower rows) and in the upper row the deceased enjoys his hobbies. He is spearing fish and shooting fowl. The fishing scene was never completed. Though the fish themselves are drawn, Nakht has no spear in hand. His wife tenderly holds an injured bird in her hand. His little daughter holds his leg to prevent him from losing balance.

It is interesting to note that, in contrast to the twelve dramatic zones of the underworld traversed by the deceased Pharaohs in their tombs in the Valley of the Kings, the deceased noblemen had simple intercourse with the gods. On each side of the entrance doorway Nakht, followed by his wife and three rows of servants, makes offerings to Amon, whose name was obliterated by Akhenaten whenever it occurred.

In the second chamber, in a shaft descending to the mummy chamber, was found a small and exquisite statue of Nakht in a kneeling position and holding an inscribed stele. This little master-piece is now lying on the floor of the Irish Sea. The s.s. *Arabic* on which it was being transported was sunk in World War I.

Nakht the man has emerged from the paintings in his tomb. We know about his official career with its emphasis on organisation, efficiency and production, his family life with its show of harmony and plenty, his entertainments with their air of light-hearted gaiety and the pastimes that gave him most pleasure.

### Tomb of Ramose (55): Plan 28

This tomb belongs to the vizier in the reigns of Amenhotep III and Amenhotep IV (later Akhenaten). It comprises a main hall with thirty-two rather squat papyrus columns (*1*), an inner hall (*2*) containing eight clustered columns of smaller dimension (all destroyed) and the shrine (*3*).

Ramose was one of the earliest converts to the sun-worship and his tomb is therefore of historical significance as one of the few standing monuments in Thebes of the period between the two faiths. It is moreover of artistic significance since it gives a unique opportunity to see conventional relief representations alongside the

**Plan 28**                                **TOMB OF RAMOSE**

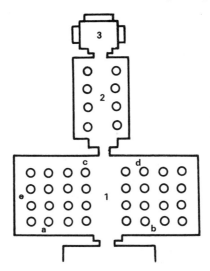

new realism which has become known as the *Amarna period*.

## The Art of the Amarna Period

Before we describe the tomb of Ramose a word should be said about Akhenaten's sun-worship and the art it heralded. The movement was not the isolated act of a rebellious Pharaoh who established a new capital in Tel el Amarna with a set of original ideas and a new outlook. The sun-worship of Akhenaten was introduced in Thebes over a number of years. The formation of a new capital, rendering Amon no more than a local deity, was really only the final step.

Light is still being shed on the transition period from one worship to another. There is considerable evidence to support the theory that Amenhotep III and his son shared a co-regency for many years at Thebes, and that, while the father was too disabled by ill-health and his son too young for the responsibility, Queen Tiy laid the foundations for the new thought that her son was to bring to fruition. Among the first steps taken were the 'enlightenment' of certain Theban noblemen to the 'truth of the Aten', and a break-away from the traditional forms of art. The tomb of Ramose dates from this period. It was started in the traditional style, continued in the new and left unfinished when Ramose followed his master to Tel el Amarna.

On both the left and right eastern walls of the main chamber, the murals are in unpainted, stylized relief. This was the conventional mural form typical of Amenhotep III's last years when his son may have been co-regent. On the southern half (*a*) Ramose the deceased vizier sits with his relatives. The men and women of his household are depicted in the traditional manner with regular faces, clothes and elaborate wigs, the details of which were carried out with fault-less precision; the only paintwork is on the eyes. On the northern wall (*b*) are scenes of worship and religious ceremonies.

The representation that most fully shows the stylized, unemotional, traditional treatment of the mural is that on the left-hand rear wall (*c*) by the central doorway. It is a portrayal of Amen-hotep IV, as he was then still called, seated below a canopy with Maat. Ramose himself is twice represented before the throne. This scene probably dates from the period of the building of the first temple to the sun at Thebes, a time when Amon was not yet openly challenged but the worship of Aten was nevertheless taking root.

However on the right-hand rear wall (*d*) we see a quite new mood. Now the young Pharaoh, who changed his name to Akhenaten only after he set up the new capital, stands with his royal consort Nefretiti on a balcony, while Ramose, depicted in Amarna style and attitude, is being decorated with gold chains. Though still in relief, one can easily recognise the new realism, especially in the portrayal of the Pharaoh and his wife. Compared with the divine incarnation of Amon at (c), here at (d) we see the Pharaoh with belly extended in unflattering truth. Above is the life-giving sun with fourteen rays. Four of them hold symbols of life and happiness. Two support his outstretched arm. Another offers the symbol of life to the nostrils of the queen. Behind is the royal bodyguard. This mural probably dates from the period just before the departure from Thebes and already the thick loins of the *Amarna period* are apparent, though some of the innovations, such as the higher relief of the attendants in comparison with the rest of the sculpture, has not yet matured. It is a preview of art movement taking shape.

Let us ponder a moment about this so-called 'freedom of artistic expression' under Akhenaten. It does not imply individualism, since the state artists worked in teams on approved themes inherited from the early dynasties. They were now freed from this traditionalism, which was encouraged by the priesthood, to do free poses encouraged by the Pharaoh. A swinging walk, relaxed comfort, tender relationships, predominate in the new art.

One theory is that the Amarna period was one of artistic degeneration. But degeneration does not take place overnight, and here in the tomb of Ramose the two art forms coexist. One may compare the stiff, unpainted, precise relief work of the earlier period with the first stages of the new realism. It is a unique opportunity to see the Pharaoh on one wall in perfect, divine immobility and, on the other, as the relaxed and physically imperfect man.

On the upper part of the left-hand wall (e) is a peculiar juxtaposition of old and new in the group of mourners, one of the most expressive and delightful drawings to be found in any tomb. Grief comes down the centuries in a heart-rending funerary convoy. The men carry boxes covered with cooling foliage, a jar of water and flowers. A group of grieving women turn towards the funeral bier, fling their arms about and throw dust in their hair, tears streaming down their cheeks. One woman is supported by a sympathetic attendant. One is so young as to be unclothed. Most of the figures are individual, expressing varied movements and degrees of grief, and are even of different sizes. But the group of five mourners at the centre of the group of women are shown as a series of parallel lines behind the front figure. Traditions are not easily broken! Further along the wall women beat their breasts and thighs in grief or squat to gather dust to scatter on their heads.

Another theory about the representations of the Amarna period is that the young Pharaoh reverted to the archaic forms of art that he held so dear. He believed that Amon was but a usurper of the true sun-worship of Ra at Heliopolis and accordingly the proportions of pre-dynastic times were recaptured. The art he encouraged, in the words of Arthur Weigall, was 'a kind of renaissance—a return to the classical period of archaic days.'[1]

In the doorway leading to the second, unfinished, chamber Ramose appears standing (on the left-hand side) and praying (on the right).

## Tomb of Khaemhet (57): Plan 29

This is the tomb of the overseer of the granaries of Upper and Lower Egypt late in the reign of Amenhotep III, a time when art and architecture were flourishing. It was also a time when religious conceptions were undergoing a gradual change towards the worship of a single deity, the sun. The murals are in low relief and are carried out in precise and sensitive detail. This is particularly apparent in the treatment of Khaemhet's wig, with his own hair showing beneath.

The tomb comprises a large traverse chamber (*1*) with a niche on the left-hand side containing badly damaged statues of the deceased and the royal scribe Imhotep, a corridor (*2*) with scenes relating to the underworld and a second traverse chamber (*3*) containing three niches bearing statues of Khaemhet and his relatives. These too are in poor condition.

On the left-hand entrance wall of the first chamber at (*a*) is a remarkable representation of Renenet, the snake-headed goddess of the granaries. She is seated in a shrine and offerings are made to her by three finely sculpted male figures. The child she nurses is symbolic of the new harvest. Further along the wall (*b*) is the bustling port of Thebes. The masts of many grain-laden vessels, the steering oars tipped with the head of the Pharaoh, the mastheads, the rigging —all are depicted in meticulous detail.

On the rear left-hand wall (*c*) is a scene showing servants of the vizier bringing in cattle. At (*d*) are damaged figures of the Pharaoh and his vizier. At the foot of the royal canopy are nine captive tribes whilst between the lion-legs of the throne are two captives: Negro and Asian.

On the right-hand rear wall (*e*) the enthroned Pharaoh (defaced) receives homage from Khaemhet and his officials. Further along (*f*)

[1] *The Life and Times of Ikhnaton*, Thornton Butterworth, 1933, page 63.

Khaemhet is being decorated by the Pharaoh; according to the inscription he was so honoured in the thirteenth year of the reign of Amenhotep III.

On the right-hand entrance wall (*g*) are a set of agricultural scenes including measuring the land, sowing and reaping. Khaemhet's chariot is drawn up near the fields and while a sleepy driver awaits the return of his master the horses take advantage of the break to graze.

In the corridor, on the left-hand side at (*h*), is a fine representation of Osiris enthroned with Hathor standing behind him.

### Tomb of Userhet, First Prophet (51): Plan 30

Although it is not in too good a state of repair, this tomb, belonging to the First Prophet of the Royal Ka of Thutmose I in the reign of Seti I, contains a symbolic scene of such high order of artistic execution that it should on no account be missed.

It is on the right-hand wall of the narrow traverse chamber (*a*) and shows Userhet and his wife and sister sitting beneath a fig-

**Plan 29**
**TOMB OF KHAEMHET**

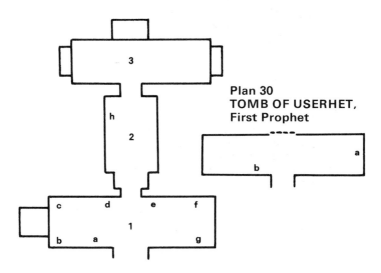

**Plan 30**
**TOMB OF USERHET,**
**First Prophet**

laden tree drinking the Water of Life presented to them by a tree-goddess who rises out of the lake before them. As the liquid is poured from a golden vessel into the cups, the three seated figures are offered figs and grapes, bread and honeycomb. The T-shaped lake between Userhet and the tree-goddess shows the souls of Userhet and his wife as human-headed birds drinking the Water of Life from their cupped hands. The symbolic purpose of the mural is almost obliterated by the imaginative and realistic treatment. It must have been a truly magnificent representation. Above the seated figures wagtails flit among the branches of the fruit-laden tree and above the two women are the human-headed birds which represent their souls or *bas*.

On the left-hand entrance wall (*b*) Userhet's heart is being weighed, not against the ostrich feather of truth, but this time against the figure of a man.

The inner corridor is in ruin.

### Tomb of Userhet, Royal Scribe (56): Plan 31
This is the tomb of the royal scribe in the reign of Amenhotep II. His name was also Userhet and the condition of his tomb is extremely good.

Rural scenes decorate the left-hand entrance wall (*a*). They include the branding of cattle and the collection of grain. On the rear left-hand wall (*b*) is a feasting scene where unfortunately all the figures of the women were destroyed by a Christian monk who made his home in the tomb. On the right-hand rear wall (*c*) men bring bags of gold-dust to be counted by supervisors (upper row), and in the lower row is a charming scene of men queuing beneath the trees to have their heads cut and shaved. The barber himself is busily at work on two clients. On the same wall (*d*) bakers are making bread (middle row) and Userhet's guests are seated (lower row). Towards the end of the wall (*e*) Userhet makes offerings to his Pharaoh, who wears a colourful red tunic with yellow spots.

The most notable scene in this tomb is on the left-hand wall of the inner corridor (*f*). It is a hunting scene in which the charioted nobleman shoots at fleeing gazelles, jackals, hares and other animals. Userhet has the reins tied around his waist and the string of his bow taut and ready to shoot. The movement among the fleeing animals is beautiful and rhythmic. Further along the wall (*g*) are scenes of fishing, fowling, and viticulture.

The right-hand wall has funerary scenes with the weeping women (*h*) beautifully depicted in their sorrow.

## Tomb of Rekhmire (100): Plan 32

Rekhmire was vizier under Thutmose III and his son Amenhotep II. The tomb follows the regular style of the 18th Dynasty nobles' tombs, comprising a narrow, oblong first chamber and a long corridor opposite the entrance. But this corridor rapidly gains in height to the rear of the tomb and runs into the rock. It was inhabited by a *felaheen* family for many years and the wall decorations have suffered at their hands. The tomb is a memorial to personal greatness and a revelation on law, taxation and numerous industries. Professor Breasted described it as 'the most important private monument of the Empire'.

Rekhmire was an outstanding vizier who was entrusted with a great many duties. There was nothing, he wrote of himself in an inscription, of which he was ignorant in heaven, on earth or in any part of the underworld. One of the most important scenes in the tomb is that on the left-hand wall of the first chamber near the corner (*a*). It shows the interior of a court of law in which tax evaders are brought to justice by the grand vizier himself. The prisoners are led up the central aisle, witnesses wait outside and at the foot of the

Hunting scene from the Tomb of Userhet.

judgement seat are four mats with rolled papyri. These indicate that written law existed in 1500 B.C. Messengers wait outside and others bow deeply as they enter the presence of the vizier.

Near the centre of the opposite wall (*b*) Rekhmire performs his dual role of receiving taxes from officials who annually came with their dues, and receiving tributes from the vassal princes of Asia, the chiefs of Nubia, etc. The foreign gift-bearers are arranged in five rows: from the Land of Punt (dark-skinned), from Crete (bearing vases of the distinctive Minoan type discovered on the island by Sir Arthur Evans), from Nubia, from Syria, and men, women and children from the South. The diverse and exotic tributes range from panthers, apes and animal skins to chariots, pearls and costly vases, to say nothing of an elephant and a bear.

The inner corridor gives an insight into the activities of the times. On the left-hand wall (*c*) Rekhmire supervises the delivery of grain, wine and cloth from the royal storehouses. He inspects carpenters, leather-workers, metal-workers and potters, who all came under his control. In the lower row is a somewhat damaged record for posterity of one of the most important tasks with which he was entrusted: supervising the construction of an entrance portal to the temple of

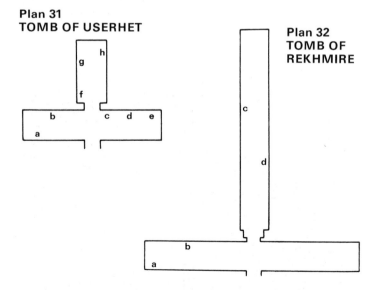

**Plan 31**
**TOMB OF USERHET**

**Plan 32**
**TOMB OF REKHMIRE**

Amon at Karnak. He held vigil over the manufacture of the raw material, the moulding of the bricks and their final use. Pylons and sphinxes, furniture and even household utensils all came under his control. There are interesting scenes, to the left of the bottom row, of seated and standing statues being given final touches by the artist before polishing. The fascinating detail provides a pictorial treatise on the different industries of the times. It is worth noting that the scene in which there are light and dark-skinned Egyptian workers making bricks for 18th-Dynasty constructions in Upper Egypt has been presented as evidence of Biblical accounts of Hebrews being used as forced labour in the city of Ramses II in Lower Egypt a century and a half later.

On the right-hand wall (*d*) Rekhmire may be seen at a table and there are traditional scenes of offerings before statues of the deceased, the deceased in a boat on a pond being towed by men on the bank, and a banquet with musicians and singers.

All the representations in this tomb show rhythm and free-posing, gesticulating and active figures. They are very different from the patterned group action with which we are familiar. The high premium traditionally set on balanced design was not lost. But the solid strings of people are gone, and with the break with the frieze the curtain is suddenly lifted on a picture of things as they really were: workers bending to mix mortar or squatting to carve a statue; a man who raises a bucket to his colleague's shoulder;

Bags of gold dust are brought to the supervisors, Tomb of Userhet.

another engrossed in carpentry; the elegant ladies of Rekhmire's household preparing for a social function with young female servants arranging their hair, anointing their limbs, bringing them jewellery. The message in these delightful murals is forceful and clear with the dignified personage of the vizier himself towering over his subordinates in administrative excellence.

### Tomb of Emunzeh (84): Plan 33

This is the tomb of the superintendent of granaries under Thutmose III and Amenhotep II. The condition is poor due largely to damage from the *felaheen* family who lived in it for many years and also due to pillage by grave-robbers.

In the traverse first chamber (*1*) on the left-hand rear wall (*a*), African tribes bring tributes including gold, panther-skins, ivory and, among the animals, a small donkey clinging to the neck of a giraffe! On the right-hand wall (*b*) Asiatics bring weapons, jars, a carriage and white and brown horses.

On the right-hand side of the rear corridor (*c*) the deceased makes

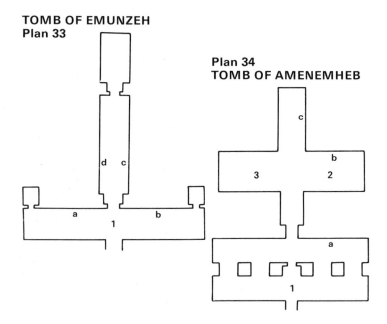

**TOMB OF EMUNZEH**
**Plan 33**

**Plan 34**
**TOMB OF AMENEMHEB**

a tour of inspection of the produce of the estate. There is a scene of the hunt for wild animals in the desert, the chase of waterfowl and the usual offering scenes, but unfortunately most of the wall is in bad condition. The funerary scenes are on the left-hand wall (*d*).

The vaulted ceiling of the shrine is finely decorated.

## Tomb of Amenemheb (85): Plan 34

This tomb has a line of pillars in the first chamber and side chambers leading off the main corridor directly behind it. It is important historically because Amenemheb was the military commander of Thutmose III, and not only does his tomb record his part in the Pharaoh's important Asiatic campaigns, but it gives exact information of the length of his reign and those of his predecessors.

Amenemheb is recorded as having accomplished two feats of unusual daring. One was during the battle of Kadesh on the Orontes when, just before the clash of arms as the opposing armies were poised and ready, the prince of Kadesh released a mare who galloped straight for the battle lines of the Egyptian army. The plan was to break up the ranks and confuse the soldiers but Commander Amenemheb, ever on the alert, reportedly leapt from his chariot, pursued the mare, caught it and promptly slew it.

The second experience took place on the return march from Asia Minor when near the Euphrates the Pharaoh was suddenly in danger of being run down by a herd of wild elephants. Amenemheb not only managed to divert the danger and save his master from a nasty fate but apparently struck off the trunk of the leader of the herd while balancing precariously between two rocks!

Naturally such a brave and dutiful warrior should be justly rewarded by his Pharaoh for his bravery and such nobles as Amenemheb received part of the booty, decorations, and in special cases even land in recognition of their services.

Three walls in this tomb are especially noteworthy. The first is in the main chamber (*1*) on the rear right-hand wall (*a*). This is the record of Thutmose III's Asiatic campaigns, his length of reign, etc., as well as a record of Amenemheb's military honours. Near the bottom of the wall Syrians bring tribute. They wear white garments with coloured braiding and there are talkative children among them.

In the chamber leading off the corridor to the right (*2*) is a scene on the left-hand wall (*b*) of a feast in progress with abundant food and drink. Servants bring bunches of flowers. The guests, relaxing in comfortable chairs or squatting on stools, are offered refreshments and the ladies in the second row all hold lotus flowers in their hands, while round their necks and in their hair they have blossoms. Attendants hold staffs wreathed and crowned with flowers. Lower on the wall are harp, flute and lute-players. It is a gay and lively representation.

In the rear corridor on the left-hand wall (*c*) is the private garden of Commander Amenemheb. Fish swim in a pool surrounded by plants. The deceased and his wife are presented with flowers.

The funerary scenes are found in the left-hand chamber (*3*) which leads off the rear corridor.

### Tomb of Sennofer (96): Plan 35

In this delightful tomb the boxed-in effect has been broken. The 'oriental tent' atmosphere of most tombs is missing because the entire ceiling has been painted with a creeping vine. Interesting use has been made of the rough surfaces of the rock to make the grapes and vine-tendrils more realistic, and the experiment has succeeded. Both the first small chamber and the main hall, which is supported by four pillars, have been decorated in this manner.

Sennofer was the overseer of the gardens of Amon under Amenhotep II. His tomb, which was excavated only in the 20th century,

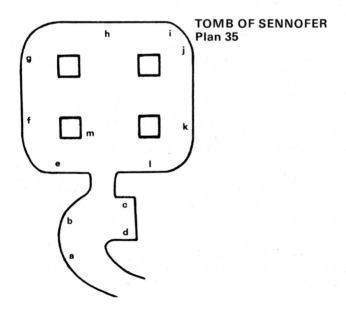

**TOMB OF SENNOFER**
**Plan 35**

Sennofer and his wife on the voyage to Abydos.

was found to have mostly religious inscriptions but the condition of the frescoes is almost perfect and their freshness and beauty make the tomb a very special one.

A steep flight of stairs takes us down to the first chamber, and the first representations we meet on the left-hand wall (*a*) show Sennofer being brought offerings from his daughter and ten priests. Circling the chamber clockwise we see on the two rear walls (*b* and *c*) drawings of the deceased with his wife worshipping Osiris who is represented above the doorway of the main chamber. On the right-hand wall (*d*) the deceased is seen entering and leaving his tomb while servants bring sacred offerings and his daughter stands behind him.

Above the doorway of the main chamber lie two representations of Anubis. Touring the chamber clockwise we come first to a scene of the deceased and his wife emerging from the tomb (*e*), and further along seated on a bench. On the left-hand wall at (*f*) are servants bringing furniture to the tomb and setting up two obelisks before the shrine. At (*g*) are funerary ceremonies and the nobleman himself (to the left) looks on. On the rear wall (*h*) the deceased and his wife are at a table of offerings while priests offer sacrifices to the dead. Further to the right (*i*) are scenes of the voyage to Abydos, statues of the deceased and his wife in a shrine in a boat being towed by another boat. Thus the deceased nobleman satisfied himself of favour with Osiris by showing that he had had the intention of performing the sacred pilgrimage.

One of the most beautiful representations is that of the deceased and his wife in an arbour (*j*) praying to Osiris and Anubis. At (*k*) a priest clad in a leopard skin purifies them with holy water and at (*l*) is the scene before a table of offerings where Sennofer puts a lotus blossom to his nostrils and his wife tenderly holds his leg.

The pillars have representations of Sennofer and his wife. Perhaps the most attractive is to be found on the left-hand pillar at (*m*).

## UPPER ENCLOSURES

### Tomb of Menna (69): Plan 36
This famous tomb of the scribe of the fields under Thutmose IV has some of the most beautiful representations to be found of harvests, feasts and hobbies. It is a fine tomb and the colours are brilliant, particularly on the ceiling of the inner chamber.

On the left-hand entrance wall (*a*) Menna can be seen before a table of offerings and further along the wall (*b*) are agricultural

The Tomb of Sennofer, Overseer of the Gardens of Amon.

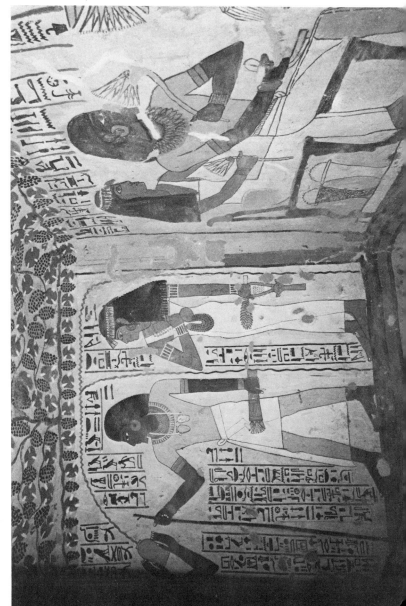

scenes with step-by-step portrayals of the grain being measured, recorded, winnowed and trodden. The ploughing and sowing is followed by reaping and, as in so many tombs, the artist has managed to add a human touch: in this case a young girl removing a thorn from a friend's foot (bottom row) and two girls quarrelling (immediately above). At (*c*) Menna stands before a ship coming in to dock with a cargo of stores.

On the left-hand wall of the rear corridor (*d*) are funerary scenes of the voyage to Abydos in fine detail and brilliant colour. Menna's heart is weighed before Osiris (the tongue of the balance has been destroyed). On the right-hand wall (*e*) is the famous fishing and fowling scene among the papyrus thickets. The deceased nobleman is enjoying his favourite pastime. Coloured fowl rise from the rushes. Crocodile, duck and assorted fish can be seen in the water. Menna's little daughter kneels to pluck a lotus flower from the rushes. The mural is a magnificent example of the importance laid on depicting good things for the hereafter. It is spoiled only by the fact that Menna's face has been carefully hacked out of the wall.

The murals of the nobles' tombs have passed through three major eras of destruction. In very early times, when ancient tomb-robbers extracted the valuable funerary equipment, the enemies of the deceased also entered the chambers to destroy some of the happy representations that the deceased wanted to repeat in the hereafter. What other reason could there be for the severing of a boomerang, the destruction of a water-jar or the blinding of the eyes?

In the Christian era when many of the tombs were used as hideouts, some of the hermits carefully plastered over the wall drawings and thus preserved them for us in excellent condition, while others scraped the distracting representations completely off the walls. At the turn of the 20th century, before proper security measures were enforced on the necropolis, antiquity dealers removed whole sections of the invaluable murals and some of the most beautiful scenes may, consequently, be seen today in many of the museums of the world.

To the right of the fishing scene (*f*) is a ship (top row) from which one of the sailors leans over the side to fill a bowl of water from the river.

On the right-hand entrance wall (*g*) it can be seen that Menna usurped this tomb. Where his stucco has fallen off, the paintings of the original owner can be seen beneath. Perhaps it was the descendants of that owner who destroyed Menna's face as an act of vengeance.

## Tomb of Intefoqer (60): Plan 37

This is a regular 12th Dynasty tomb comprising a long entrance corridor before the main chamber. It belongs to the governor and vizier under Sesostris I and is one of the oldest tombs in this group. It is situated high on the mountain and commands a good view of the Nile Valley.

In contrast with the 18th Dynasty murals, these paintings are somewhat crude and carried out on rough plaster. They are nevertheless quaint and informative. On the right-hand wall of the main chamber (*a*) is a hunting scene with the deceased shooting game in an enclosure. The gazelles, hares, etc. are being chased by dogs. Birds are being netted and fish are being hauled in from a square pond of water. Just beyond the centre of the wall (*b*) is a series of cooking scenes and still further along (*c*) is a representation of Intefoqer and his wife.

Towards the centre of the left-hand wall (*d*) is a fascinating representation of a funerary dance. It takes place before the deceased is brought to the tomb. The male performers have unusual reed crowns. They chant 'O Hathor—a newcomer' and 'She has inclined her head', the second chant indicating approval by the goddess of the deceased's entry to the underworld.

The inner chamber has a deep niche at the end, designed to hold Intefoqer's statue (which has now been reconstructed). The burial

**TOMB OF MENNA    Plan 36**

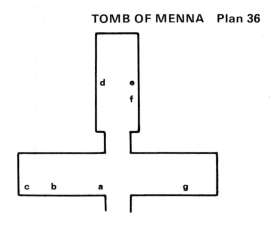

shaft extends off this chamber. On the right-hand entrance wall (*e*) are musicians, both male and female. The offerings to the gods of the underworld are near the centre of the right-hand wall (*f*).

### Tomb of Haremhab (78): Plan 38
This nobleman was royal scribe, scribe of recruits and the official in charge of revenue in the reigns of Thutmose III, Amenhotep II, Thutmose IV and Amenhotep III. He should not be confused with the Pharaoh of the same name. His tomb comprises a traverse hall and a single long corridor.

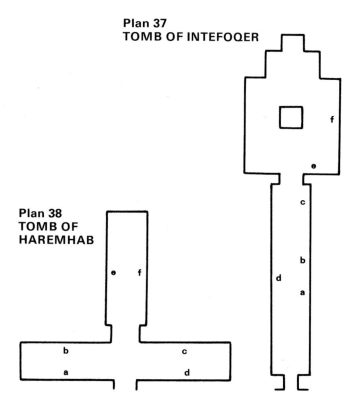

**Plan 37**
**TOMB OF INTEFOQER**

**Plan 38**
**TOMB OF HAREMHAB**

Nakht and his family enjoy fishing and fowling in the hereafter.

# 162

On the left-hand entrance wall (*a*) the much damaged figures of Haremhab and his wife are being offered bowls by servants as female musicians play to them. On the left-hand rear wall (*b*) the deceased (obliterated) presents to the Pharaoh the contributions of the peasants. Above this scene are scribes registering the peasants who are arranged in groups headed by standard bearers. On the right-hand wall (*c*) foreign tributes are brought in by plumed Asiatics. Note that a group of negroes from the Sudan are women (upper row) who carry their babies in the well-known negro fashion, tied to their backs. On the lower wall is a gay scene of negroes dancing to a drum beat. On the right-hand entrance wall (*d*) is the familiar funerary feast with dancing and music.

The left-hand wall of the inner corridor (*e*) has the traditional funerary scenes. On the right-hand wall (*f*) is a much damaged fishing and fowling scene.

## Tomb of Ineni (Enne) (81): Plan 39

This was the architect who excavated the first tomb in the Valley of the Kings, that of Thutmose I. His tomb comprises a main chamber, the façade of which is formed of pillars which carry their murals on the rear faces, and a corridor.

Three of the square pillars carry particularly interesting murals. The first (*a*) is a hunting scene with a rearing hyena biting a broken

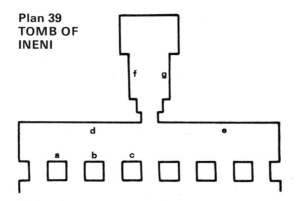

Plan 39
TOMB OF
INENI

Thoth weighs the heart of the deceased against a figure of the Goddess of Justice and Truth, Tomb of Menna.

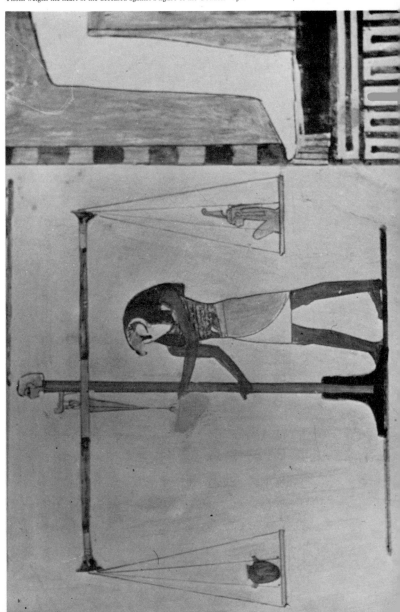

arrow as a dog rushes the wounded creature from the rear and gazelles flee. The second (*b*) shows Ineni's country house and he and his wife are seen in the arbour (damaged) from whence he orders his gardener round the walled estate. On the third pillar (*c*) Ineni can be seen before a sumptuous feast.

On the left-hand rear wall of the first chamber (*d*) Ineni receives tributes from swarthy Nubians including two women who carry their babies on their backs (top row). Below he receives contributions from the peasants. This part of the mural is squared up for the draughtsman. On the right-hand wall (*e*) is a scene in poor condition of Ineni and his pet dog watching a parade of the estate animals including sheep, goats, flamingoes and geese.

On the left-hand wall of the rear corridor (*f*) Ineni and his wife receive offerings. On the right-hand wall (*g*) are more funerary scenes and offerings. The roof is decorated.

In the niche at the rear are four seated statues of the deceased and his wife.

## Plan 40
## TOMB OF MENKHEPERRASONB

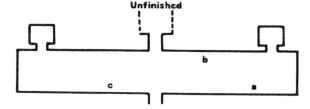

### Tomb of Menkheperrasonb (86): Plan 40

This tomb was never completed. Only the regular traverse chamber was constructed and this has two small chambers projecting from the rear walls on either side. It belonged to the first prophet of Amon in the reign of Thutmose III, who was another of those masters-of-all in ancient Egypt who could as readily turn their hands to agriculture as to raising an obelisk.

Towards the end of the right-hand entrance wall (*a*) craftsmen are at work on weapons, vases, etc., while gold for the inlay is being weighed out (upper reaches). The inscription records for posterity the fact that the illustrious Pharaoh Thutmose III actually designed some of the vessels himself, thus creating a precedent followed by several monarchs and statesmen!

On the right-hand rear wall (*b*) foreign envoys bring gifts ranging from gold and silver inlaid vases to diverse weapons, battledress and horses. The negroes wear loincloths, the Syrians their traditional braided robes. Having extended his empire Thutmose III was thus recorded as having homage paid him by the chieftains of Kheftiu, the Hittites, Tunip and Kadesh.

The left-hand entrance wall (*c*) has harvest scenes.

# ASASIF

### Tomb of Kheru-ef (192): Plan 41

The tomb of Kheru-ef, which was closed to visitors for many years due to reconstruction, is now open.

Kheru-ef was steward to the Great Royal Wife Queen Tiy at the crucial period of the 18th Dynasty just before Amon was dethroned by Akhenaten. The tomb was never completed but the murals are carved in exquisite high relief.

The outer courtyard contains various other tombs and a wall has been constructed to preserve the reliefs of Kheru-ef. On the left-hand wall are delightful scenes from the Sed festival, the 30-year Jubilee of the Pharaoh. Amenhotep III and Queen Tiy are seated with Hathor behind them (*a*) watching a processional dance in their honour. Further along the wall (*b*) they leave the palace with eight slim princesses walking in pairs and bearing jars of sacred water. At (*c*) delightful carvings of the ceremonial dance suggest a ritual of rebirth of life on the earth and include a jumping bird, a flying bird and a monkey. In the lower row are musicians with flutes and drums. Towards the end of the wall (*d*) is a sketch of the high priest and the text describes the celebration.

The right-hand section of the wall is somewhat damaged. At (*e*) Amenhotep III is portrayed with his sixteen princes. With Queen

# 166

Tiy he watches the erection of a column symbolising the god Osiris (*f*). At (*g*) the Pharaoh and Queen Tiy are shown with the deceased nobleman behind them. Beneath the trio are the conquered cities.

The other nobleman of this era, when the royal capital was being shifted to Tel el Amarna, was Ramose. But while Ramose followed his master to the new capital, Kheru-ef remained in Thebes with the royal mother.

**Plan 41**
**TOMB OF KHERU-EF**

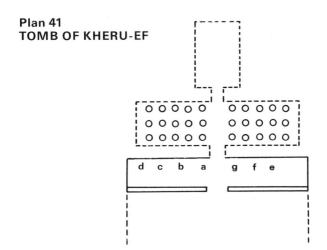

## DEIR EL MEDINA

These tombs, which mostly date to the 19th and 20th Dynasties, were built by the workmen employed in the Valley of the Kings (page 70/71). The most well known are:

### Tomb of Sennudjem (1): Plan 42
This is the tomb of the Servant in the Place of Truth in the early Ramesside period. The mural decoration, which had not yet developed that stiffness that characterised the later Ramesside period, is in extremely good condition and the low curved roof is used to continue the themes of the side walls.

A narrow flight of stairs, followed by a curved flight, leads to this entrance of the tomb. On the wall opposite the doorway (from left to right) are: (*a*) Anubis embalming the mummy of the deceased, (*b*) Osiris before an offering table flanked by two Horus eyes, (*c*) offerings and perfumes and (*d*) the deceased being led by Anubis.

On the right-hand wall (*e*) is an agricultural scene with ripe wheat fields, fruits and flowers. In the lower row are ploughing scenes. On the opposite wall (*f*) is a delightful representation of the deceased nobleman and his wife, whose transparent dress reveals slender limbs.

On the roof are scenes of the opening of the door of the tomb, the journey to the underworld and chapters from the Book of the Dead as well as the tree of life and the sacred spotted Apis bull.

On the left-hand side of the doorway (*g*) is a scene showing the mummy of the deceased in the tomb with Nephthys and Isis in the form of birds and (lower row) the wife and daughter of the deceased. On the right-hand wall (*h*) are evil spirits and (lower row) the deceased and his family.

In this tomb one feels an intense intimacy with the deceased as he was during his life and as he carried his treasures and pleasures to his grave. Perhaps it is the fine condition of the murals that helps to create this feeling. Perhaps, and more likely, it is the very smallness of the tomb itself.

**Plan 42**          **TOMB OF SENNUDJEM**

### Tomb of Pashedu (3)

This is another well-preserved and decorated tomb of the Ramasside era. On the *right hand* entrance wall the owner, the servant of the Place of Truth, is depicted crouching in prayer by a decorative palm-tree that grows beside a lake. The religious themes inside the tomb are similar in style to those of Sennudjem.

### Tomb of Inherkhau (359)

This tomb is one of the finest examples of 20th Dynasty art to be found. It dates to the reigns of Ramses II and IV, and the owner was the artistic supervisor of the necropolis. He was therefore in charge of a team of artists and craftsmen, and there is little wonder that he took special care of his own tomb.

The side walls of the innermost chamber contain the most excellent scenes, each in three registers. On the *right-hand* wall Inherkhau can be seen adoring two lions, guardians of the two horizons which came to represent Today and Tomorrow. There is also a charming scene of the deceased with a group of his grandchildren, receiving a statuette of Osiris, and a box containing a *Shawbti* figure. On the *left-hand* wall are scenes showing the deceased worshipping a lotus and the Horus-Hawk (with a cat killing a snake beneath the sacred tree). Inherkhau is also shown with his wife holding candles and listening to a harp-player.

### Tomb of Ipuy (217)

This tomb, or rather shrine, belongs to a sculptor in the reign of Ramses II. The drawings, which are rapid sketches, are unusual, if not unique. The tomb is divided into two wings. In the *right-hand wing* the most interesting scenes are on the right-hand wall, where all aspects of rural life can be seen, from farming, fishing and snaring to market scenes and the cooking of poultry and fish. On the rear wall craftsmen make funerary furniture and equipment.

The *left-hand wing* has a much faded but interesting scene towards the centre of the left-hand wall: a house and garden (note the *shaduf*, one of the most ancient of pumping devices) and laundry scenes.

It was from the tomb of Ipuy that a marvellous relief depicting the grape harvest and wine-press was hacked out of the wall towards the end of the 1930s. In fact the problem of desecration of monuments and illicit digging continues to be a most serious one, as outlined in our concluding chapter.

Scene from Tomb of Sennudjem showing wheat fields, fruits and flowers in the hereafter.

CHAPTER 9
THE TEMPLE OF DEIR EL MEDINA

**The Temple of Deir el Medina: Plan 43**
This small, graceful Ptolemaic temple, completely surrounded by
a brick wall, lies in a barren hollow and was dedicated to Hathor and
Maat. It took shape under the Ptolemies. Within its precincts Christian monks built a monastery the remains of which can be seen to
the left and right of the temple. It was these monks who gave it its
name.

Deir el Medina is often overlooked by visitors in favour of the
larger, more impressive monuments. This is a pity as it is a temple
of considerable beauty and in an excellent state of repair. It is
thought to have originally been founded by the architectural genius
under Amenhotep III, known as Amenhotep son of Hapu, who, like
the architect Imhotep, builder of Zoser's Step Pyramid, was
deified in Ptolemaic times. In fact, there are two representations, of
Imhotep and Amenhotep son of Hapu, on the pillars at the end of
the screen wall separating the two parts of the building.

The temple consists of a large vestibule (*1*) containing two
elaborately adorned palm-columns with floral capitals and a screen
wall dividing it from a central hall (*2*) and the back of the temple
where there are three shrines. Here, as in so many temples in the
Nile valley, the pure lines of Egyptian work and the elaborated
Graeco-Egyptian style are found side by side.

Passing through the entrance doorway of the temple we notice
steep rocks. The façade, which has a hollow cornice, bears names
which attest to the many Copts and Greeks who visited the temple.
Facing us are the two palm columns and behind them the screen
walls with pillars bearing heads of Hathor. Near the top of the wall
on the left is a window which once lighted a staircase.

In the left-hand shrine on the left-hand wall (*a*) is a chapter from
the Book of the Dead showing Osiris seated (near the end of the wall)
and before him four genii of the dead upon a lotus flower. Thoth
inscribes the verdict. To the left the heart of the deceased
(Philopator) is weighed by Anubis and Horus in one of the most

complete representations of this scene to be found, and also one of the most beautiful. With the 42 judges of the dead (upper row) the deceased is led to the scene of the judgement by Maat who, in another representation and joined by Anubis and Horus, weighs the heart of the deceased against the feather of truth. Note that Anubis and Horus not only measure the weight but test the scales; Horus himself checks the balance; Thoth records the result. If it proves satisfactory then the deceased enters the underworld, if unsatisfactory he will be devoured by the hippopotamus-like monster before him.

On the rear wall (*b*) the deceased offers incense to Osiris and Isis. On the right-hand wall (*c*) is the sacred boat with standards, etc. Above the doorway (*d*) is a four-headed ram representing the God of the Four Winds and above this strange creature a flying vulture worshipped by four goddesses. On the jambs of the doorway the Pharaoh is represented with three hawk-headed and three jackal-headed genii.

In the centre shrine (*3*) are representations of the deceased before the various Theban deities.

In the right-hand shrine on the right-hand wall (*e*) are fine carvings of seated deities: Osiris with Hathor, Isis, Horus, Nephthys and Anubis behind him. On the left-hand wall (*f*) are Mut, Amon-Ra, etc.

South of the temple of Deir el Medina is the settlement of tomb and temple workers (page 70). The cemetery lies to the west.

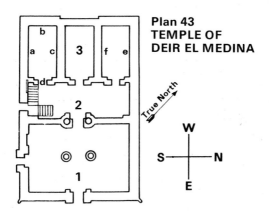

**Plan 43**
**TEMPLE OF**
**DEIR EL MEDINA**

---

## CHAPTER 10    A PLEA FOR LUXOR

---

The legendary 'hundred-gated Thebes' is in danger. The threat comes from three sources: contamination, desecration and abuse. That is to say, environmental contamination from humidity and sub-soil water, plunder by grave robbers, and injury by tourists.

It may come as a surprise to know that Luxor is endangered at all. We tend to think that the great temples and magnificent tombs will endure, for the simple reason that they have already survived for thousands of years. This is a fallacy. During the nine years since this book was first published, damage is not merely perceptible, but, in many cases, unmistakable.

*Environmental contamination:*
It was at first thought that the High Dam at Aswan, the cornerstone of the country's economic development envisioned by Nasser and built during the years 1960–71, had improved conditions for the conservation of monuments. The stabilization of the river was regarded as a boon, since it overcame the danger of high floods. This, it was thought, would enable the reinforcement of undermined foundations and prevent further collapse of large structures. Furthermore, it was reasoned that the injury caused to some monuments by the excessive wetting and drying out each year, would be ended.

It is now clear that the higher average water-table damages reliefs through seepage and salt erosion, which are even more serious. While the annual flood had totally destroyed reliefs on the lower reaches of the temple walls, the parts above flood level were, considering their age, well preserved. Now the seepage and salt erosion are causing progressive deterioration of the reliefs on the upper walls as well.

Archeological teams working in Luxor (see Work in Progress) are well aware of the danger, and, for many years, have combined excavation and documentation with reconstruction and conservation. The Franco-Egyptian Centre at Karnak, particularly, have concentrated their efforts on the latter problem. Specialists working for the Centre have carried out experiments over many years. As a result of their studies, many previously held views have had to be revised; for example, the misconception that damage was caused through subterranean seepage alone, and that there was no humidity in Upper Egypt. Indeed, there is. Moreover, methods of conservation that have proved to be successful on monuments in other parts of the world have proved less so in Egypt. Here the natural process of evaporation of moisture must be allowed, but crystallisation be curbed.

Experiments take time. Seasons pass. Time takes its toll. And the decay creeps up the temple walls like some cursed disease, leaving the reliefs pimpled, festered and spoiled.

*Plunder:*
Tomb robbing is not new. So long as there have been tombs there have been robbers; even in Pharaonic times. Before the foundation of the Antiquities Department in 1850 (at first administered by the French under Mariette), 'plundering excavations' resulted in great collections of Egyptian antiquities around the world, especially in France, Britain, Turin, Florence, Bologne and Leydon. The last fifty years, however, has seen some of the most vicious desecration of monuments ever known. Large portions of decorated wall relief have been literally hammered away in order to remove a chosen scene or figure. The tomb of Ipuy (page 168), suffered this fate, and also the crypts of the Temple of Hathor at Dendera, to mention but two.

The tragedy of modern-day plunder is that the antiquities are lost to the world of art and scholarship, as they too often make their way out of the country, through antique dealers, and into private collections. The Egyptian government have clamped down on illicit digging, and have seized hordes of rare antiquities before they could be smuggled out of the country. In a recent coup on the Theban necropolis, they caught a robber before the damage was done. This occurred in February 1981. The would-be thief had excavated a tunnel twenty metres long and four metres beneath ground level, from his home in the foothills of the necropolis, towards the tomb he intended to plunder. When he emerged, he found the police waiting for him.

The problem is serious. There are hundreds of tombs on the necropolis that spread over an extensive area. The Egyptian architect Hassan Fathi thought he had one possible solution when he designed and built a model village twenty-five years ago. After a careful study of the requirements of the community on the necropolis, it was designed on traditional lines with domed sun-dried brick buildings and with every facility including pens for livestock, local school, and mosque. The idea was to attract the people who lived in hovels atop the honeycomb of tombs at Kurna to a more attractive and healthy environment, and subsequently to implement control of the tombs. When the first stage of the project was completed, however, the people refused to budge. The model housing was never occupied, the project was abandoned, and tomb robbing continues.

Needless to say, it is impossible to curb illicit digging and desecration until the monuments have been identified. Here it is heartening to know that the necropolis is being scientifically mapped by Kent Weeks, in what has become known as the Berkeley Theban Mapping project (see No. 4 below). It is undoubtedly one of the most important projects in Luxor today; for, only when the study is complete and the sites identified, can proper control be implemented, and pillage curtailed.

*Injury by tourists:*
Tourists are destroying the monuments. This is no idle statement. The tomb of Seti I in the Valley of the Kings was temporarily closed for reasons described on page 120. Unless something is done, others will suffer the same fate, for tourism is rapidly increasing. It is estimated that the new airport at Luxor will handle two thousand visitors a day; that is, of course, apart from those arriving by train, river, bus and car. To facilitate their movement to the necropolis, it is planned to build a bridge over the Nile.[1]

Needless to say, the time is long overdue to take action. To build a terminal for the rumbling buses at a safe distance from the tombs, and to construct rest-house facilities where drainage will not affect the tombs hewn out of porous limestone bedrock in the Valley of the Kings, are two high priority projects. No less important, however, is the need to establish ground-rules for tourists, such as strict batching according to the size of the tomb. The companies that organise package tours often have little concept of the distances involved, or the time needed to see a monument. As a result there is a constant fight against time. Tour leaders often transport their groups in busloads of forty. Anxious to keep them intact, and happy, they hustle them, too many at a time, into a tiny nobleman's tomb, or urge them to enter the priceless corridors of the royal tombs before an earlier group has emerged.

[1] As this third edition goes to press it has been learned that this project has been abandoned in order to preserve the natural beauty of Luxor.

Alternative itineraries would certainly ease pressure. Open more tombs and circulate the people. For example, the Tomb of Tutankhamon could be linked with that of Merenptah (as a traditional tomb) and Ramses IV (which was used by Champollion during his stay in the Valley of the Kings).

The tomb of Amenhotep II, the most beautiful in the valley, could be linked with that of Ramses VI (famous for its 'Golden Hall') and Ramses III ('Tomb of the Harpists').

The Tomb of Haremhab, the most popular during the time the Tomb of Seti I was closed, because of its size, high quality reliefs (some unfinished), and magnificent tomb chamber with sarcophagus, could be linked with the remote tomb of Thutmose III (the empire builder) and Ramses IX (as a classical tomb).

The alarm has been sounded. Let it not pass unheeded. It will *not* be all the same a hundred years hence.


## WORK IN PROGRESS IN LUXOR

1. The Austrian Archeological Institute has been clearing and restoring tombs in the Asasif area for many seasons and continue to do so. In 1976 they discovered the hitherto unknown tomb of Ankh-Hor, which dates to the 26th Dynasty. Due to the poor quality of the rock, the ancient sculptors had first cut limestone blocks that they fitted to the walls, before decorating them. The tomb has now been published.

2. The Belgian Archeological team continue to clear and document tombs, also in the Asasif area. Towards the end of the 1976/77 season they came across a large part of a badly damaged Saitic tomb (26th Dynasty), belonging to Padi-Horresnet. During subsequent seasons, more parts of the tomb came to light. Restoration is now in progress and a publication is on the way.

3. An archeological team from the Brooklyn Museum in New York are excavating the Temple of Mut at Karnak. A survey was started in 1976 under the directorship of Richard Fazzini, and the first season of digging, in 1977, was rewarded with success. Portions of a temple were exposed, a monumental gateway built by Taharka, the Kushite king (25th Dynasty) was excavated, as well as some mud-brick houses. James Manning, associate director of excavations, is confident that work on the temple will cast light on the origins of the cult of Mut, and on

such questions as Mut's identification with the goddess Sekhmet (consort of the great god Ptah of Memphis).

Another team from the Brooklyn Museum, carrying out a brief survey in the Valley of the Kings with a view to ascertaining the feasibility of recording undocumented tombs, found some foundation deposits at three corners of a fifteen-metre shaft in the Tomb of Ramses XI. Among the pieces excavated were statuettes, about eight inches (20.5 cm) high, of two figures: the king with the royal uraeus on his forehead, and the goddess Maat with the feather of Truth.

4. The University of California at Berkeley started the first scientific mapping of the necropolis under Kent R. Weeks in 1978. The last map of the necropolis dates to 1921 and it was incomplete even then. The first season started with detailed measurements and recording of all known tombs, mapping their positions and subterranean contours, with the aid of the most sophisticated surveying equipment. During the second season, air-photographs were taken with the collaboration of the Egyptian Academy of Science. Work continued (unusually) throughout the summer of 1980, when the team completed the first stage of a three-dimensional map of the Valley of the Kings; and 1981, when they moved ahead to do a similar study of the Valley of the Queens.

5. The University of Chicago's Epigraphic Survey of the Oriental Institute is now in the final stages of fieldwork in recording the processional colonnade, the great *Opet* festival, of Luxor Temple; reconstruction of the numerous fragments forming new scenes will follow. At Medinet Habu, documentation of the great Mortuary Temple of Ramses III has now been completed and published, and the expedition will concentrate its activities on other structures within the complex, dating from periods earlier and later than the Ramses III temple: A small temple of Amon, the construction of which dates from the reign of Hatshepsut (18th Dynasty) and continued through to the Roman period; and the chapels of the Saite Princesses (25–26th Dynasty). Also scheduled for the coming season is documentation of the tomb of Nefer-sekheru, No. 107, at Sheikh Abd el Kurna.

Lanny Bell, Director of Chicago House in Luxor, enumerates the publications either in press, or in the final stages of editing (in 1981): *Khonsu II, The Battle Reliefs of Seti I at Karnak, Khonsu III* (the architecture in collaboration with the Franco-

Egyptian Centre at Karnak), Harold H. Nelson's copies of the reliefs and texts on the inner walls of the Great Hypostyle Hall at Karnak, and the first plate volume of William J. Murnane's edition (in collaboration with the Epigraphic Survey and the Franco Egyptian Centre at Karnak.). The beautiful reliefs of the Tomb of Kheru-ef, (on which clearance and documentation started in 1956) are now published in a work by Ch. Nims, L. Habachi and Ed. Wente.

6. The Egyptian Centre for Documentation, in collaboration with UNESCO represented by Mme. Christianne Desrouches-Noblecourt and French assistants, continue to excavate and document the Ramasseum, the Mortuary temple of Ramses II. While working in the Valley of the Queens during the 1978 season, they located some of the little-known tombs, such as the Tomb of Towy, mother of Ramses II, and also the tomb of Princess Meritamen, one of Ramses II's favourite daughters.

7. The Franco-Egyptian Centre at Karnak, sponsored by the Egyptian Government and the Centre of Research for France (CNRS), under Professor Claude Golvin, ended a decade of research and reconstruction in 1980. Hundreds of *talatat* from the Sun Temples of Akhenaten are still being excavated from the 9th Pylon of Haremhab; these blocks can easily be reassembled in the manner of the three hundred-odd blocks now exhibited in Luxor Museum, as they were buried in the order in which the temple was dismantled.

In the 1979/80 season, an almost complete shrine of Sesostris I came to light; it was one of the most exciting discoveries at Karnak in recent years. As already mentioned, the Franco-Egyptian Centre at Karnak has been actively engaged in studies on the progressive deterioration of monuments through water seepage, humidity and salt erosion.

8. The French Institute of Oriental Archeology, under Professor Jean Vercoutter, has recently celebrated its centenary; one hundred years of excavation in Egypt. At Karnak north, Jean and Helen Jacquet, architect and egyptologist respectively, have just completed a ten-year study (1968 to 1978), which resulted in the discovery of a treasury from the time of Thutmose I. The results will be published in a multi-volume work that will cover all aspects of their study: stratigraphic, architectural, epigraphic and descriptive.

The French Institute's sixty-year long study of the Worker's village and tombs at Deir el Medina (pages 70/71) has already resulted in scores of publications, which have added significantly to our understanding of the activities and attitudes of the people involved in excavating and decorating the royal tombs in the Valley of the Kings. The team, under the directorship of Jean Vercoutter will continue to clear, document, reconstruct, interpret and publish the results of their work.

9. The German Archeological Institute have been carrying out various projects, including some in the area of Luxor, for well over a decade. On the necropolis their activities have been concentrated on the Mortuary Temple of Mentuhotep the Great; and in the El Taref area, the northernmost point of the necropolis where the princes of the 11th Dynasty were buried, Professor Arnold heads excavations.

While excavating the former site, the Mortuary Temple of Mentuhotep, some foundation deposits were found at the four corners of the so-called pyramid. These proved to be a rare and complete collection of samples of all the implements used by architects at the time, in addition to some tiny tablets, and long pieces of linen, dating from the erection of the monument (*c.* 2134 B.C.), and even earlier. Reconstruction continues, and successive publications have already appeared.

In a trial project in the 1975/76 season, the German Institute, under Professor Stadelmann, applied a photogrammetry technique for the documentation of reliefs in the Mortuary temple of Seti I at Kurna. The technique, hitherto applied to document architecture and, in fact, used for the restoration and relocation of the temples of Abu Simbel, was successful. By using a process of stereoscope photography and special apparatus, a three-dimensional, undistorted picture of the subject is projected. This rapidly speeds up the process of documentation and, subsequently, publication.

10. The Italian archeologists are active at two sites in Luxor: The University of Piza's mission is headed by Professor Bresciani. While excavating the area of the Mortuary Temple of Thutmose IV on the necropolis, the house of the temple's architect was located. This is a rare specimen of a private building from the New Kingdom. They also found a rare shrine of the Ramses' period, and a grave of the Middle Kingdom. The latter was later (in the New Kingdom) reused as a store for ceramic materials.

The University of Roma, under Professor Donadoni, has been working on the tomb of Sheshonk of the Libyan (Late) Period. Reconstruction nears completion and a publication is in press.

11. A Japanese archeological team, which started excavations to the south of Malqatta, south-west of Medinet Habu in the 1976/77 season, discovered a staircase forming part of the *Heb-Sed* Court of Amenhotep III. They are now searching for pre-dynastic settlements on the Theban necropolis, and are beginning to record some of the tombs of the nobles.

12. The Universities of Pennsylvania and Toronto, having found the ground plan of one of the Sun Temples of Akhenaten (page 62), will continue to excavate to the east of the great Temple of Amon-Ra at Karnak. Professor Redford maintains that the temple will probably prove to have been built around a 200 to 300-metre courtyard, surrounded by rectangular pillars, before each of which were huge statues of Akhenaten. The statues, twenty-four in number, were originally found around the same area by the French archeologist Chevrier, in 1925, when a drain of about five metres was dug to reduce the subsoil water that accumulated in the temple for part of the year.

13. The Polish Archeological Institute will continue the massive project of restoration above the third terrace of Queen Hatshepsut's Mortuary Temple at Deir el Bahri, where they discovered a temple of Thutmose III. Hundreds of blocks and statues have been found. From the blocks, and from plaster casts of blocks from the same temple that were taken to the Metropolitan Museum in New York between the years 1911–1931, they plan to reconstruct a large part of the temple.

   The Polish Institute have also illuminated the Temple of Queen Hatshepsut, to enable visitors to appreciate the beauties of ancient Egyptian architecture by night.

14. The Swiss Institute of Archeology have been working on the Mortuary Temple of Amenhotep III, the largest on the necropolis, for the last decade. They have discovered numerous statues of deities that were erected within the temple, and have identified parts of the monument which were plundered and taken all over the world, even to Leningrad, early in the century. A publication by H. Ricke, L. Habachi and G. Haeny has now appeared.

   Work on the adjacent Temple of Merenptah continues. This temple is particularly interesting because blocks from various other monuments were reused in its construction, including some from the Mortuary Temple of Amenhotep III.

# 180

## LUXOR MUSEUM

The Museum at Luxor, opened in March 1976, is situated on the river's edge about half-way between the great temples of Luxor and Karnak. It has been designed by one of Egypt's leading architects Mahmoud el Hakim to display works of art from three main sources: from the temples of Luxor and Karnak, from storehouses containing treasures excavated from both sides of the Nile in Luxor, and some selected pieces from the Cairo Museum. The Brooklyn Museum was consulted regarding the selection of objects, and was also active, in an advisory capacity, in their installation.

Visitors to this air-conditioned Museum, on two levels under a single roof (a ramp leads to the upper gallery), will be attracted by effectively illuminated works of art, offset against near-black walls. The creation of individual vistas at strategic positions encourages an organised, uninterrupted flow of people through the Museum, and prevents the tendency to double back and congest the space.

The first focal point is the recently found red granite head of Sesostris I, followed by a well to the right, where the magnificent gold-leaf head of the cow-goddess, Hathor, from Tutankhamon's tomb, is displayed. Effective lighting encourages visitors to make their way to the stairway to the rear of the main hall, which leads to a long gallery flanked by displayed objects.

After the major work of art and the major relief, the next focal point is the magnificent alabaster statue of Amenhotep III, seated beside, and under the protection of, Sobek, the Crocodile-god. This, the largest free standing statue in the Museum, is half-way up the gallery. In approaching it visitors pass on the right the famous stele narrating how Kamose conquered the Hyksos (page 37), and various other works of art from the Theban area on the left.

From the centre of the gallery, attention is drawn once more towards illuminated objects at the end of the gallery, where a ramp leads to the upper floor and commands an excellent view of the lower gallery.

The first important work of art on the upper floor is one of the two famous statues of Amenhotep, son of Hapu; it is individually illuminated. On the short wall are some blocks, carved in relief, from the famous quartzite shrine of Hatshepsut, taken from the restricted area of Karnak Temple (see Plan 4); and, as one makes the turn, one's attention is immediately drawn to the two heads of the Pharaoh Akhenaten which introduce the Amarna Period (pages 144/145).

On the upper gallery of Luxor Museum is one of the finest reconstructions of modern times: the famous 'Akhenaten Wall', an 18-metre wall reconstructed from 300 of the 6,000 blocks of Akhenaten's Sun Temple extracted by the Franco-Egyptian Centre at Karnak from Haremhab's ninth pylon (page 60). The wall is a record of some aspects of everyday life during the period of sun worship and has been so constructed that newly-discovered or identified pieces can be systematically added to the wall.

A display area for small objects, such as jewellery, faience vessels and items of adornment, is situated immediately above the circular display area on the ground floor. The second ramp leads the visitors downwards towards the entrance hall, past Coptic reliefs.

One of the unique features of Luxor Museum is the huge slab, or slatted wall, along its outer face, which separates and enhances the building proper. This serves to keep the Museum cool and creates, at the same time, a colonnade where statues are displayed and illuminated at night. Several large stone works are exhibited in the grounds of the Museum also, as for example the famous stele of Amenhotep II, one of the finest single examples of relief (photo on page 65).

Another important feature of the Museum, apart from the various storage areas, offices, reference library and study areas, is the Staging Area where the majority of works of art are prepared for mounting and cleaning. The ticket-booth leads to an outdoor cafeteria overlooking the Nile on the south side of the Museum.

## HISTORICAL OUTLINE

The division of Egypt's history into royal dynasties from the time of Menes to Alexander the Great was the work of an Egyptian priest, Manetho (280 B.C.). Although this grouping was subsequently combined into what is generally known as the *Old Kingdom* or Pyramid Age, the *Middle Kingdom* and the *New Kingdom*, modern historians, though their opinions differ considerably, have further divided it thus:

Predynastic Period *c*. 5000–3100 B.C.
Early Dynastic Period
  (1st and 2nd Dynasties) *c*. 3100–2686 B.C.
Old Kingdom
  (3rd to 6th Dynasties) *c*. 2686–2181 B.C.
First Intermediate Period
  (7th to early 11th Dynasties) *c*. 2181–2133 B.C.
Middle Kingdom
  (11th and 12th Dynasties) *c*. 2133–1786 B.C.
Second Intermediate Period
  (13th to 17th Dynasties) *c*. 1786–1567 B.C.
New Kingdom
  (18th to 20th Dynasties) *c*. 1567–1080 B.C.
Period of Decline or Third Intermediate Period
  (21st to 24th Dynasties) *c*. 1080–715 B.C.
Late Period:
  (25th Dynasty—Kushite) *c*. 750–656 B.C.
  (26th Dynasty—Saitic) *c*. 664–525 B.C.
  (27th to 30th Dynasties—mostly Persian) 525–332 B.C.

## TABLE OF THE MOST IMPORTANT KINGS FROM THE RISE OF THEBES TO THE GREEK CONQUEST

*The lengths of the various reigns shown below are approximate:*

## MIDDLE KINGDOM: 11th–12th Dynasties (2133–1786 B.C.)

The Middle Kingdom was the second of Egypt's three 'great periods' and a time of great building activity. The Old Kingdom, or Pyramid Age, had collapsed in anarchy and bloodshed, but after about two centuries of strife, power was seized in Upper Egypt by a family from the area of Luxor. A series of leaders by the name of Intef and Mentuhotep gradually succeeded in reuniting the country.

**Mentuhotep III**
50 years

Mentuhotep the Great was the first pharaoh of a re-united Upper and Lower Egypt. During his long reign he laid down strong foundations for the 12th Dynasty.

**12th DYNASTY**
**Amenemhet I**
30 years

He was the founder of the 12th Dynasty in whose reign peace was restored. Though he and his successors were natives of Luxor, they established their capital in the Fayoum region.

**Sesostris I**
**(Senusert I)**
45 years

He was the son of Amenemhet I, who shared a co-regency with his father for ten years, and continued his policies after his death. This continued also during the reigns of his successors Amenemhet II and Sesostris II.

**Sesostris III**
**(Senusert III)**
33 years

Sesostris III was the most powerful pharaoh of the dynasty. He managed to further suppress the power of the local lords and strengthen centralised control. He conquered Nubia and later became deified there.

**Amenemhet III**
45 years

He reclaimed land from Lake Fayoum and established a rich and prosperous province in Middle Egypt.

**Amenemhet IV**
13 years

There is indication of a breakdown in the central government towards the end of his reign.

**Second Intermediate Period: 13th–17th Dynasties (1786–1567 B.C.)**

Egypt was governed by a succession of kings, many of whom were named Sobekhotep, but it was a period of decline and finally the country was conquered by the Hyksos. These tribes came from the direction of Syria, swept down the Nile valley with their horses and chariots, leaving death and destruction in their path, and subjecting Egypt to the humiliation of foreign occupation.

## NEW KINGDOM: 18th–20th DYNASTIES
## 18th DYNASTY (1567–1320 B.C.)

**Ahmose I**
22 years

He was the brother of Kamose who fought to liberate Egypt from the hated barbarian tribes, the Hyksos. Ahmose I continued the war of liberation.

**Amenhotep I**
10 years

As he had no son to inherit, the throne fell to a relative, Thutmose I, who had married Amenhotep I's sister.

**Thutmose I**
30 years

He was the first Pharaoh to construct a rock-hewn tomb in the Valley of the Kings. While he was still alive a struggle took place between his three children: Hatshepsut (the only child of direct royal lineage via her mother the Great Royal Wife) and her two brothers (by lesser wives).

**Thutmose II**
**Hatshepsut**
**Thutmose III**
54 years
altogether

Hatshepsut built a magnificent mortuary temple and encouraged trade and architecture. She reigned concurrently with Thutmose II, whom she married doubtless to keep the crown within the royal family. For a time Thutmose III also ruled jointly with her. When eventually he asserted his sole rule he proved militarily the ablest of the Pharaohs, establishing Egyptian influence throughout Asia Minor, Nubia and Libya, thus creating an Egyptian world empire.

**Amenhotep II**
26 years

The son of Thutmose III, Amenhotep II followed his father's policy, going twice to Syria in his reign. As a young man he was known for his extraordinary muscular strength.

**Thutmose IV**
8 years

While resting in the shade of the Sphinx at Giza he dreamed that his father Amenhotep II ordered him to release him from the sand and promised that Thutmose would become king if he did so. Thutmose IV was a good sportsman like his father.

**Amenhotep III**
36 years

Known as *Amenhotep the Magnificent*, he was the Pharaoh who reaped the benefits of the conquests of his predecessors. Thebes was at the peak of its glory during his long rule.

**Akhenaten**
**Amenhotep IV**
20 years
approximately

Amenhotep III's son Amenhotep IV was later known as Akhenaten. He started a religious revolution, transferred the royal residence to Tel el Amarna and worshipped a single deity, the sun, in place of the numerous deities hitherto worshipped. He was particularly hostile to Amon, chief god of Thebes.

**Smenkare**
10 years
approximately

He was co-regent with Akhenaten during the last years of his reign.

**Tutankhamon**
9 years
approximately

The boy-king Tutankhamon restored the worship of Amon and transferred the capital back to Thebes.

**Ay**
4 years
approximately

After Tutankhamon's sudden death his tutor Ay married the boy-king's widow and briefly succeeded to the throne.

**Haremhab**
34 years

This general who seized the throne was the first Pharaoh of non-royal lineage. An excellent administrator, he re-established strong government for the first time since Amenhotep III some sixty years earlier.

The 18th Dynasty, which lasted at least 230 years, emerged as a long awaited liberation from foreign rule, achieved strong government, a foreign empire, expansive trade and an artistic and architectural revolution. But it ended in a halting recovery from a religious setback that affected Egypt's standing abroad more than at home and which in the long run was to prove a turning point in her history.

## RAMESSIDE PERIOD: 19th–20th Dynasties (1320–1080 B.C.)

### 19th DYNASTY

**Ramses I**
2 years

He transferred the capital to the Delta.

**Seti I**
21 years

He fought the Libyans, Syrians and Hittites. But the empire was growing weaker. He encouraged an artistic revival most notably in his temples at Kurna and Abydos.

| | |
|---|---|
| **Ramses II**<br>67 years | Hero of a war against the Hittites, with whom he signed a famous peace treaty, Ramses II was a celebrated builder of great monuments. But he ruled an ever-weakening state. |
| **Merneptah**<br>10 years | Although of advanced years when he succeeded his father Ramses II, Merneptah was also warlike. He sent his armies to Syria and fought a bitter battle against the Libyans in the fifth year of his reign. |
| **Amenmesis**<br>**Merneptah-**<br>**Siptah**<br>20 years<br>approximately | These two successors of Merneptah were of little consequence, though the latter did gain ascendancy in Nubia. |
| **Seti II**<br>2 years | He tried in his short reign to maintain foreign prestige and internal security. But Egypt's decline continued. |

## 20th DYNASTY

| | |
|---|---|
| **Setnakht**<br>1 year | He restored order after the five years' reign of a Syrian usurper. |
| **Ramses III**<br>31 years | The last Ramses of any consequence, he conquered the Libyans and repelled invaders. |
| **Ramses IV**<br>to<br>**Ramses XII** | During this period the state gradually fell to pieces. Finally the powerful state priesthood under Hrihor seized the throne and overthrew the dynasty. |

## PERIOD OF DECLINE: 21st–24th Dynasties (1080–715 B.C.)

This was a period of decline. The theocratic government became synonymous with corruption and a state of semi-anarchy prevailed. Nubia became independent and Egypt lost control of Palestine. In the 22nd Dynasty a family from Herakleopolis Magna ruled for some two centuries. They were of Libyan descent but completely Egyptianised, and carried out many building enterprises.

## 25th DYNASTY (750–656 B.C.)

**Taharka**
25 years

This was the Kushite Dynasty, ruled by a strong family from the northern Sudan who presented themselves as true Pharaohs, having long absorbed the customs and traditions of Egypt. During Taharka's rule the ancient Egyptian culture was reimbued with vigour. The Assyrian conquest put an end to Kushite rule.

## 26th DYNASTY (664–525 B.C.)

**Psamtik**
54 years

The 26th Dynasty is known as the Saite Period, or Saite Revival, when noblemen from the Delta managed to reunite the country and set it on a sound economic basis.

## 27th–30th DYNASTIES (525–332 B.C.)

There were two Persian conquests during this period. Though the Persians claimed to be genuine Pharaohs, and found favour with the bulk of the population, there were several revolts against their rule.

**Nektanebos II**
18 years

This was the last Egyptian pharaoh to carry out constructions before the Greek conquest of 332 B.C.

When Alexander the Great marched on Egypt 332 B.C., the Egyptians had no reason to believe that this would be the beginning of the end of their status as an independent nation. For a time under the gifted Ptolemaic rulers, the country became once more a rich, powerful and prosperous state, but later the Ptolemaic rule was characterised by decadence and fratricidal wars. After the Roman occupation 30 B.C., Egypt was no more than a dependency of Rome, and although the appearance of a national Egyptian state was maintained, and the Romans continued to build and adorn temples, there was a steady drain on the country's resources.

Christianity was introduced to Egypt during the Roman era.

# SUGGESTIONS FOR FURTHER READING

ADAMS, WILLIAM Y. *Nubia, Corridor to Africa*, Allen Lane, London, 1977.

BREASTED, JAMES, *A History of Egypt*, Hodder & Stoughton, London, 1950.

FRANKFORT, J *Ancient Egyptian Religion; an interpretation*, Harper, New York, 1961.

GARDINER, SIR ALAN, *Egypt of the Pharaohs*, Oxford University Press, 1961.

HABACHI, LABIB, *The Obelisks of Egypt*. Charles Scribner's Sons, New York, and J. M. Dent, London, 1977.

KAMIL, JILL. *Upper Egypt: Historical Outline and Descriptive Guide*, Longman, London, 1983.

*Sakkara; a Guide to the Necropolis and the site of Memphis*, Longman, London 1978.

*The Ancient Egyptians; How they Lived and Worked*. David and Charles, Newton Abbot 1976.

KEES, H. *Ancient Egypt; a Cultural Topography*. Faber & Faber, London, 1961.

KEATING, R. *Nubian Rescue*, Robert Hale, London, and Hawthorn Books, New York, 1975.

LUXOR MUSEUM OF ANCIENT EGYPTIAN ART *Catalogue* American Research Center in Egypt, Cairo, 1979.

MURNANE, W. J. *United with Eternity: a concise guide to the monuments of Medinet Habu*, American University of Cairo Press, Cairo, 1979.

# INDEX*

---

\* This Index does not include every name that appears in the text; obscure deities are not included, nor those place names, such as Ashmounein and Coptos, which appear once and serve no purpose for reference.

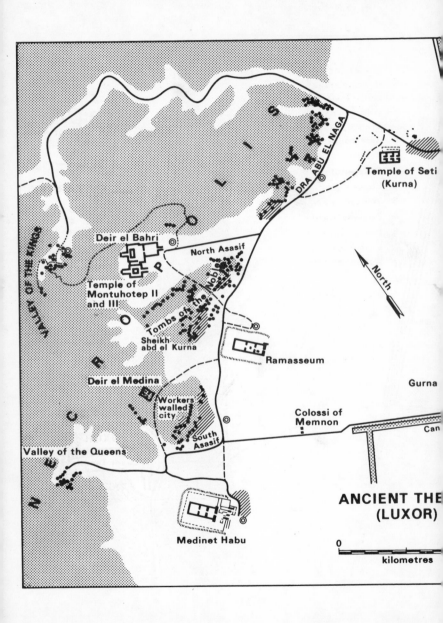

VALLEY OF THE KINGS

DRA ABU EL NAGA

Temple of Seti
(Kurna)

Deir el Bahri

North Asasif

North

Temple of
Montuhotep II
and III

Tombs of the Nobles

Ramasseum

Sheikh
abd el Kurna

Deir el Medina

Gurna

Workers
walled
city

Colossi of
Memnon

South
Asasif

Can

Valley of the Queens

ANCIENT THE
(LUXOR)

Medinet Habu

0

kilometres